Teaching With

# BIBLE GAMES

## *Twenty*
### "Kid-Tested" Contests to Make Christian Education Fun

# ED DUNLOP

Meriwether Publishing Ltd.
Colorado Springs, Colorado

**Meriwether Publishing Ltd., Publisher**
**Box 7710**
**Colorado Springs, CO 80933**

**Editor: Rhonda Wray**
**Typesetting: Sharon E. Garlock**
**Cover design: Tom Myers**
**Interior photographs: Norman Abshire, Rick Brooks, Pastor Harold Coe, Evangelist Dale Grisso, Louise Petersen, Gary Pruett, Jerry Short**
**Pattern illustrations: Beth Tallakson**

All Scripture is taken from the King James Version.

**Library of Congress Cataloging-in-Publication Data**

Dunlop, Ed, 1955-
    Teaching with Bible games : twenty "kid-tested" contests to make Christian education fun / by Ed Dunlop. -- 1st ed.
        p.        cm.
    ISBN 0-916260-94-1
    1. Christian education of children. 2. Bible games and puzzles.
3. Flannelgraphs.     I. Title.
BV1475.2.D86   1993
268'.432--dc20                                                     93-16857
                                                                          CIP

## DEDICATION

*To Janice —
my wife, best friend,
and faithful source of encouragement.*

# TABLE OF CONTENTS

**PART ONE**
*The What, Why and How of Bible Games* . . . . . . . . . .   1

Introduction . . . . . . . . . . . . . . . . . . . . . . . . . . . . . . . . .   3

Why Teach With Bible Games? . . . . . . . . . . . . . . . . . . . . .   7

Using Bible Games Effectively . . . . . . . . . . . . . . . . . . . . .   15

Game Boards and Materials . . . . . . . . . . . . . . . . . . . . . . .   23

**PART TWO**
*Twenty Bible Games to Make*
*Christian Education Fun* . . . . . . . . . . . . . . . . . . . . . . . .   29

Zonk! . . . . . . . . . . . . . . . . . . . . . . . . . . . . . . . . . . . . .   33

Rabbit Hunt . . . . . . . . . . . . . . . . . . . . . . . . . . . . . . . . .   39

Survival . . . . . . . . . . . . . . . . . . . . . . . . . . . . . . . . . . . .   43

Matchmaker . . . . . . . . . . . . . . . . . . . . . . . . . . . . . . . . .   49

Dinosaur Daze . . . . . . . . . . . . . . . . . . . . . . . . . . . . . . . .   53

Leap Frog . . . . . . . . . . . . . . . . . . . . . . . . . . . . . . . . . . .   59

Double Dip . . . . . . . . . . . . . . . . . . . . . . . . . . . . . . . . . .   63

Sea Monster . . . . . . . . . . . . . . . . . . . . . . . . . . . . . . . . .   67

Sky War . . . . . . . . . . . . . . . . . . . . . . . . . . . . . . . . . . . .   71

The Lost Dutchman . . . . . . . . . . . . . . . . . . . . . . . . . . . .   75

Magic Squares . . . . . . . . . . . . . . . . . . . . . . . . . . . . . . . .   81

Clown Toss . . . . . . . . . . . . . . . . . . . . . . . . . . . . . . . . . .   85

Good Guys and Bad Guys . . . . . . . . . . . . . . . . . . . . . . . .   89

The Green Machine . . . . . . . . . . . . . . . . . . . . . . . . . . . .   93

Green Machine Baseball .......................... 99

Bible Treasure ................................. 103

Busy Bees .................................... 107

Build-A-Bug .................................. 111

Hungry Bears ................................. 115

Chasing Butterflies ............................. 119

**PART THREE**
***Sample Questions From the Bible*** ................ 123

**PART FOUR**
***Patterns*** ..................................... 167

**A FINAL WORD** ............................... 209

# PART ONE

## *The What, Why and How of Bible Games*

# Introduction

As you teach the Sunday School lesson, your restless Juniors steal frequent glances at the clock on the wall. It ticks off the minutes ever so slowly. Finally, you close your Bible and announce, "That's all for today. Now let's review."

"Aw, do we have to? I hate to review!"

"We just heard the lesson; why do we need to review it?"

But wait! Today is different! Instead of saying, "Let's review," face your students with a look of excitement and announce, "Today we're going to play a game! It's called *Zonk!* Boys against the girls! Who's going to win?"

That same crowd of disinterested, bored children is going to come alive! You won't believe the enthusiasm and excitement! As the students leave your class today, you'll hear comments like, "Wow! That was awesome! Can we play *Zonk!* again next week?"

If you are a minister, Christian education director, Vacation Bible School or Sunday School teacher, I challenge you to begin using Bible games in your teaching opportunities. Your class time will sparkle with a new life. Teach with Bible games in Sunday School and Junior Church, in training hour, and in your backyard Bible club. Use them in your Wednesday evening club program, and even in your Christian school. Once you start teaching with Bible games, you'll wonder how you ever made it without them.

Bible games are a ton of fun, and an excellent learning experience for your students. They can be used with almost any age group, including Beginners (four- and five-year-olds), Primaries (first, second, and third graders), Juniors (fourth, fifth, and sixth graders), and Junior High students. Use the simpler games with the younger children, and the more complicated ones with the sophisticated Junior High students. (I've even used them on occasion with High School students.)

Bible games can be used with almost any size group of youngsters. I've used them with six kids, and I've used them with crowds of over 600 kids!

This book will get you started. It contains ideas for 20 games that we have developed during 16 years of full-time ministry with children. Each of these games has been thoroughly "kid-tested." They're winners with the kids! Each game in this book has been used time after time, in all sorts of teaching situations, with large groups and small. You'll find that they work!

So, read the book, dash out to get some poster board, felt, Velcro, and other supplies, and then start making your first Bible game! Today! Then use it for the first time — this week! Your students will love you for it.

If you develop some Bible games ideas of your own, and they work well with your group of children, be sure to send them on to me. We've got dozens of games that we've used successfully over the years, but we're always looking for new ideas. And who knows? Maybe your idea will appear in our next book of Bible games!

# Why Teach With Bible Games?

It all started about 16 years ago, almost by accident, really. I had just graduated from Bible college and was working in my first church — a small congregation in southern California. I was the assistant pastor, but most of my duties in the church were with the children's ministries.

One Sunday morning, Dawn Boone, a beautiful little eight-year-old, came into Junior Church carrying a box. She approached me with a pleading look in her eyes.

"Mr. Ed," she said, "I got a Bible game for my birthday! Could we play it today in Junior Church? Please?"

I opened the box. It was *Bible Tic-Tac-Toe*. The grid for the game had been printed on a piece of plastic like a tablecloth. Forks and knives were supposed to be used for the Xs and Os. Dawn had even brought the forks and knives.

"Could we play it today? Please?" Dawn begged again.

"Maybe," I halfway promised her. "If we have time."

After the Bible lesson, we spent the last few minutes of Junior Church playing *Bible Tic-Tac-Toe*. I noticed that the kids responded with unusual enthusiasm. When class was over, I asked Dawn if she would bring her game again next week. We played the game the next two Sundays. The children loved it! And not only did they have fun, but they learned biblical concepts as well.

The kids' excitement was contagious and prompted me to invent other Bible games to use in Children's Church. My first Bible game was *Bible Football*. One Sunday morning, before the kids arrived, I drew a giant football gridiron on the chalkboard. Ten-yard lines were marked off, and I drew a football on the 50-yard line. When the girls answered a Bible question correctly, the ball was erased, and moved ten yards toward the girls' goal. If the boys answered a question, the ball was moved toward their goal. When a touchdown was scored, you would have thought we were at the Super Bowl.

The game was very well-received by the kids, so in just a

few weeks, we made a permanent game board for it. The playing field was of green felt, 3' x 6'. The white lines on the field were made with white first-aid tape. We hung it on the wall in Junior Church and played it many times.

But that was just the beginning. Today, some 16 years later, we have made and used several dozen different Bible games. We have used Bible games at camps, in Christian school chapels, and in Sunday School and Junior Church. We have used them in Christian gatherings for kids, like Awana and backyard Good News Clubs, and in Kids' Crusades in many different states. We've used Bible games in just about every teaching situation you can think of.

I believe in using games to teach and review God's Word. If you teach children, you can use Bible games. Your students will look forward to your class if these simple games are a part of your teaching program.

Perhaps you've never used a Bible game in your children's ministry. Let me give you several reasons why they are so effective in teaching God's Word to young people:

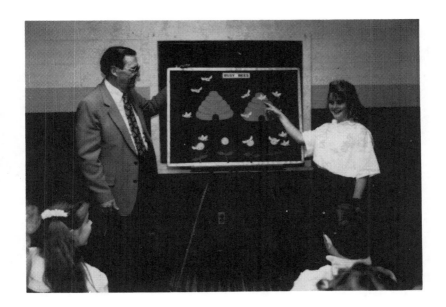

### *Bible Games Make Learning Fun and Exciting!*

Do your students enjoy your class? Do they look forward to it each week? Many times, when I talk with kids, I find that they think of Sunday School and church as being dull and boring. Where would they get that idea? The sad truth is, many times our Sunday School class or Junior Church is just that. Dull and boring.

For many years, people seemed to think that education was a lot like medicine. You know, the worse it tasted, the better it was for you! But, researchers have discovered that the best learning situations are those where the student enjoys being there.

Why should we ever bore a child when we are teaching him the Word of God? Find ways to make your class interesting and exciting! Bible games can bring that kind of life to your teaching situation.

### *Bible Games Encourage Participation*

Every class seems to have at least one Joe Cool. Or maybe in your class, it's Josephine Cool. You know, the kid that sits in the back row, never sings, never knows the memory verse, never participates in any way. You wonder why he or she even comes to class.

But, watch your Joe Cool when you start a Bible game! Joe will just sit there for the first question or two, watching. But, on the third or fourth question — SURPRISE! Joe's hand shoots up! He's actually participating!

I have seen, in one situation after another, children who would not participate in any way during Sunday School or Junior Church get involved in the Bible game. A carry-over benefit is that they became involved in every other part of class time also.

There are a couple of things to keep in mind the first

time that Joe responds during a Bible game. First, don't show surprise when Joe responds, and second, be sure to call on him. If you do not call on Joe when he responds, after a few questions he will quit trying. And then you've lost him.

### Bible Games Involve the Entire Class

Bible games can be used with just about any size group of children, large or small. I've seen crowds of several hundred kids play a Bible game. And the entire group was involved!

When you play a Bible game with your group of students, address each question to the entire group, then allow one student to answer. Each student in the entire class will frame the answer to your question in his or her own mind, hoping to be the one you call on to answer.

### Bible Games Are an Excellent Method of Review

Do you as a teacher understand the importance of review in your teaching situation? The educators tell us that one-third of our teaching time should be spent in review! Think of that! One-third! If you have a 30-minute teaching period, 20 minutes should be spent teaching new material, with 10 minutes set aside for review. If you have a 45-minute class to teach, you should spend 15 minutes of it in review. That's pretty heavy, isn't it?

Review is so very important, yet so many times we don't even plan *any* time for review as we teach God's Word.

Perhaps in the past your attempts at review have been met by such comments as, "Why do we have to listen to this again? We just heard this!"

Don't announce "Let's review!" and then wait for the inevitable groans of dismay. Instead, why not announce "Today we're going to play *Sea Monster*!" and then watch the students respond with enthusiasm. Bible games will quickly become your favorite method of review!

### Bible Games Help to Evaluate Our Teaching

Have you ever walked out of class thinking, "Now that lesson went well; my students really listened!"? And then you meet one of your students in the hall who asks a question that shows she didn't understand your lesson at all!

Many times we as teachers think that we have taught one thing, when in reality, our students have learned something entirely different! One of the weaknesses of teaching is that we have to depend on words to convey our thoughts to our students. And words can have so many different meanings, and they can be so easily misunderstood!

Bible games give us an opportunity to find out, in the students' own words, just what they are learning from us.

I remember that once in Junior Church, a little girl responded with a very strange answer to one of the questions in the Bible game. I thought, "Now, where was she? We just covered that in the lesson!" I repeated the question and called on a boy to answer. He gave me an answer almost identical to the girl's! I called on a third child, and got the same answer! Suddenly I realized that I had not presented the Bible truth quite as clearly as I thought I had.

Bible games give you an opportunity to get verbal feedback from your students, which you can use to evaluate your teaching.

### *Bible Games May Be Used to Stress Important Points*

After you have taught the lesson, use your Bible game to re-emphasize the important points of that lesson.

How do you do that? Simply write your questions out in advance, drawing many of the questions from the main points of application in your Bible story or lesson.

When I first started using Bible games over 16 years ago, I would ask general Bible knowledge questions. "How many books are there in the Bible?" "What is the first book in the New Testament?" "What are the names of the four Gospels?", etc. Then I began to see that the Bible games could be used to review and re-emphasize the lesson. We've used Bible games that way ever since.

If you teach boys and girls, I trust that you'll begin using Bible games this week. You'll soon be as excited about using them as I am. And you'll soon agree that they are a very exciting and effective teaching tool! Your students will love your class!

In the next chapter, I'll show you some ways to use Bible games most effectively.

# Using Bible Games Effectively

Let's look at some ways to make the most effective use of Bible games in your teaching situation.

A Bible game may be used at the beginning of the class session to review a previous lesson or series of lessons from a previous quarter. In our own experience, however, we have found it most effective to use the Bible game at the close of the class time to review the lesson that had just been taught.

Briefly, here's how a Bible game is played. At the close of your lesson, announce the Bible game for the day. Explain the rules for the game.

Designate one of your students as the "starter" for the game. (The "starter" will honk a bicycle horn, ring a counter bell, or strike a note on the piano after each question as the signal for the other students to respond to your question.)

When the students stand in response to the starter's signal, you, or one of your adult workers acting as "spotter," choose the child who responded first after the signal. (Note that it is usually best not to allow a child to be the game spotter.) If that student can answer your question correctly, he comes to the flannelboard or Velcro board to play the game and try for points for his team.

The teams may be divided up in a number of ways. One note of caution: *do not* appoint child captains to pick and choose the teams. This elitist method destroys the self-esteem of the last few kids to be chosen. Bible games are not a popularity contest. The objective is to include *all* kids. The teams may simply be boys against girls (you'll find some fierce competition here), or the children may number off, or you may divide your class by grade levels, age, or whatever method is quickest and easiest for you. Don't spend much time dividing your teams.

If the child who responds cannot answer your question, or answers incorrectly, repeat the question and choose another student to answer. This second student may be from the same team or from the other team — whichever you choose.

You'll find that it works best for an adult to keep score. When the game is finished, announce the score, and lead the winning team in a quick cheer.

Here are a few rules to follow in using Bible games:

## Make Bible Games Fun and Exciting!

Approach the game time with enthusiasm and a note of excitement in your voice. Relax your class behavior rules ever so slightly during the game. Allow the students to cheer for their team when they score points. You should be just as excited as the students when they score points, and just as disappointed when they don't. When you announce the winning team at the end of the game, make it extra-special by posting either the girls' or boys' blue ribbon prize on the board. The pattern may be found on page 208. Use blue poster board and laminate and attach Velcro to the back. Use your enthusiasm and creativity to make the Bible game the most exciting part of the class period.

## Ask Questions That are Easy to Understand

There is no need for trick questions during a Bible game. Consider your objectives in playing a Bible game with your

16

students: to review the lesson and evaluate your students' comprehension of it, to re-emphasize the main points and deepen the impression made by the lesson, and to have the opportunity to correct wrong impressions.

There is an art to writing good questions. I used to work with a man in a Junior Church in Phoenix, Arizona, who could word questions in a way that was remarkably clear and concise. When I discovered that his questions were so much better than mine, we put his talent to use. I would have him sit in the back during Junior Church and write questions from the message for the Bible game which was to follow.

Write out your questions for the Bible game in advance, and keep them simple and concise. See Part IV for sample questions.

### Ask Questions That Relate to the Lesson

The Bible game is far more than just a fun time or a time-filler. Use it to review the Bible lesson. Always ask questions that relate to the lesson that you have just taught, or to a series of lessons that you have taught.

Let's say that your lesson for the day has been from Genesis 3: the story of the Fall, and how sin entered the world. You would then draw each of your questions from Genesis 3, perhaps with a few questions reviewing the story of Creation in Genesis 1 and 2.

### Use Both Factual and Bible Truth Questions

Your Bible game questions should be of two types — those that deal with the facts of the Bible story, and those that deal with the application of the story.

Back to the lesson from Genesis 3. You'll probably use questions that deal just with the facts stated in the Scripture text: Who were the first man and woman? What was the name of the garden where God placed them? What was the one thing that God told Adam and Eve not to do?

Then you'll want to ask questions that deal with the application, or what I'm calling Bible truth questions: Why did God tell Adam and Eve not to eat of the fruit of the tree? Why did they disobey God? What are the results of their sin? How does sin hurt us today?

Again, write your questions in advance. Poorly worded questions are confusing to the children and will not accomplish your objectives.

### Address Questions to the Entire Class

Always ask the question first, then direct it to one team or to a particular student. Each of your students will then frame the answer in her own mind before you call on one student to answer.

### Accept Only Correct Answers

This is vital. There will be times when you are tempted to accept an incorrect answer so that a particular child will have an opportunity to play the game. But remember, if you accept an incorrect answer, you are teaching your class that the answer was correct!

Always be gracious to the child who gives an incorrect answer. Never allow the other students to ridicule the boy or girl who gives an incorrect answer. Smile at the student as you inform him gently that the answer was incorrect. Then allow another child to answer.

### *Repeat the Correct Answer So That All Can Hear*

Remember that you are teaching Bible truths as you play the game, and you want the entire class to hear the correct answer. This is more important than the scoring of points in the game.

You'll have that shy little girl in the front row who whispers her answer so that you can barely hear it. Be assured that most of the class missed her answer. Before she comes up to play the game, repeat her answer for the rest of the class.

On occasion, you will ask a question that no one in the class will be able to answer, even when you rephrase it. Be sure to give the correct answer before you go on to the next question.

### *Don't Allow One or Two Students to Answer Every Question*

Every Sunday School class seems to have at least one student that knows the answer to every question you ask, and wants to be allowed to answer every question. You, or the adult spotter that you designate, need to allow that student to answer a question during the Bible game, but then make sure that all the other students also have a chance to participate.

Be sure to choose children from the front of the room to answer questions, as well as the kids in the back. Choose kids from the sides of the room, and kids in the middle. Let the younger children participate, and be sure not to overlook the older ones. What I'm saying is this — get the entire group involved! You would not believe how many times I have had a game spotter who chose only the kids in the front row, question after question. If that happens, ask the spotter to choose children from the other sections of the room as well.

### Set a Time Limit

Bible games are exciting, but be sure to quit before the interest lags. It is always best to stop the game while the students are still enjoying it and wanting more.

I usually suggest about a dozen questions for the game. Ten or 12 questions, plus the time at the game board, will usually involve about 10 to 12 minutes of class time. Even if you do have plenty of class time, you do not want the game to go for 20 or 25 minutes.

Always plan to finish the game while the interest level of the students is still high.

### Use a Variety of Games

I related to you that our first Bible game was *Bible Football*. The children seemed to really enjoy it, so we played it week after week, month after month. I guess we played it nearly every week for almost six months! Finally I began to realize that the kids were losing interest. In fact, at that point, there was almost no interest. The kids had simply grown tired of *Bible Football*.

I began to devise some new games to keep the children from getting bored. After awhile, I had a variety of options. Now we play a Bible game in Sunday School or Junior Church for only two weeks, then go on to a new game. We put the old game away for a year or so, and when we get it out, the students are excited about it again.

This book contains ideas for 20 Bible games that you can make. Get the materials and make your first game this week. Use it in class for the next couple of weeks and, while you are using that first game, you can be working on your next game.

One more thing. If the boys have won a particular game one week, and the girls win the next week, go ahead and play the same game for the third week. Plan for a very exciting tie-breaker game!

Simply announce, "The girls won *Leap Frog* today, and the boys won it last week! Next week will be the championship game! Which team is going to win the championship game next week?" Needless to say, the *Leap Frog* championship game will be very exciting!

I trust that you are already excited about using your first Bible game. Let's look at some ideas for building the game board and making the games, and then we'll get into the actual game plans.

# Game Boards and Materials

When making the board to be used for the Bible games, you will want to consider the size of the group of children you will be teaching.

We have used game boards of two basic sizes. The first is the standard flannelboard, 27" x 36". I suggest using this size board with groups of up to 40 children. It can be used with slightly larger groups, but it's not as effective as the giant board.

The giant board is 4' x 8', the size of a full sheet of plywood. This size board can be used effectively with crowds of several hundred kids, both as a flannelgraph board for the Bible lesson and as a game board. I would use this size with any group of 50 kids or more.

The smaller of the boards (27" x 36") can be very versatile if you make it from Marlite. Go to a building supply store and purchase a 4' x 8' sheet of Marlite (white board), the type that is used as paneling in bathrooms, etc. Have someone cut it with a table saw into 27" x 36" pieces. Save the smaller pieces, as they may be used as little "walkie-talkie" boards — that is, small pieces of Marlite (roughly 12" x 16") that Sunday School teachers may carry to use for visual aids as they walk about the classroom and teach their students.

Once your board is cut to size, spread white craft glue thinly and evenly across the brown surface of the board or use a spray adhesive. Lay flannel across the board, and allow the glue to dry.

Trim the excess flannel around the edges of the board. The board can now be trimmed with silver duct tape, or you can have someone make an aluminum frame for it.

You now have a double-duty visual board, with a flannel-board surface on one side, and a white dry-marker surface on the other! Dry-markers may be purchased at any office supply store.

The giant board can be made from a full sheet of half-inch plywood and mounted permanently to the wall in your classroom or, for portability, it can be hinged in the middle and supported by two sturdy easels.

As you did with the smaller board, spread craft glue thinly and evenly across the surface of the board. Allow it to dry slightly, then lay the fabric across the board, trimming the excess after the material is on the board. Again, the board may be trimmed out with duct tape, or have someone in your church make an aluminum or wooden frame for it.

For either size board, you can choose one of two fabrics. Flannel works well, as flannelgraph figures or pieces of felt will stick to it. The board must be leaning at a slight angle, as it would if placed on an easel. If the board is completely vertical, as it would be if mounted on a wall, the figures will sometimes fall to the floor.

The second (and in my opinion, better) choice is to use Herculon, or a Herculon-type fabric. You simply put Velcro (the hook side) on the back of your flannel figures or game pieces, and the figures will not fall off!

My giant board utilizes Herculon and Velcro. Once, while I was speaking at a camp in Arizona, the wind blew the board off the easels and slammed it face down on the concrete. When we picked up the board, every figure was still in place! Try that with a flannelgraph!

Any fabric store that carries upholstery fabrics should have Herculon, or a Herculon-type fabric. You want it in a solid color, of course. Dark colors make your story figures and Bible games look their best. Take a piece of Velcro and actually test the fabric before you buy it. You should hear that distinctive "Velcro sound" when you pull the Velcro from the fabric.

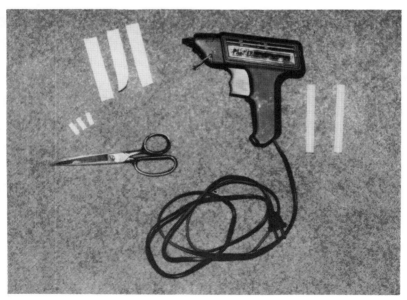

*Some needed supplies:*
*Scissors, Velcro strips, and a hot glue gun.*

25

Velcro can be easily attached to the back of your flannel figures and game pieces. Simply glue a couple of small pieces to the backs of flannel figures, or sew it to the backs of felt pieces. If your game pieces or visuals are laminated, fasten the Velcro to the back with hot glue. (The lamination plastic is usually very slick, so it is best to use a piece of sandpaper to roughen the spots where you plan to attach the Velcro.)

The Velcro will grip the visual board so well that you can use it to attach heavier objects to your board, such as bottles, books, and even bricks! Try that with a flannelgraph!

The various parts of the Bible games can be made from poster board (do not use construction paper, as it fades quickly) or felt. Some of the games pictured in this book were made from ready-made bulletin board aids, available at any school supply store.

If the figures or Bible game pieces are made from poster board or the professionally printed bulletin board aids, be sure to laminate them for durability and waterproofing. If a heat laminating machine is not available to you, you can laminate the figures at home, using clear Contact paper. Contact paper is usually thicker and more durable than the heat lamination, anyway.

To laminate with Contact paper, try this procedure. Peel the paper backing off the piece of Contact paper that has been cut to a size slightly larger than the visual or game piece to be laminated. Lay the Contact paper, sticky side up, on your work table. Then lay your visual or game piece face down on the Contact paper.

Cut a second piece of Contact paper, peel the backing, and lay it on the table, sticky side up. Then lay the visual, one side already laminated, on top of this piece of Contact paper.

Gently smooth out the lamination to remove any air bubbles, and trim the visual with scissors, leaving about a quarter of an inch of plastic around the outside edges. Visuals laminated in this way will last for years.

Just a word regarding the storage of your Bible games. If you are going to take the time to make them, then you also want to take the time to store them properly, so they will last for many years of usage.

The games for the smaller board will usually fit into a letter-size file folder. Cut the tab off the folder, and then it will fit into a 9" x 12" manila envelope. Label the envelope with the name of the game, and then store it in any file cabinet. Games stored this way should last for years. I still have our original games from years ago.

For the giant games, it is very easy to make your own storage envelopes. Two pieces of white poster board are needed for each envelope.

Fold the first piece of poster board in half, so that the two sections measure 22" x 13", and 22" x 15". One side is 2" longer than the other, so fold this extra 2" over to form the flap of the envelope. Staple the two 13" sides closed, and then tape them with duct tape. You now have a sturdy envelope, 13" x 22". The flap of the envelope may be fastened closed with Velcro.

Cut the second piece of poster board to measure 21" x 25". Fold this piece in half. You now have a folder measuring

12½" x 21". Place your game pieces into the folder, slip the folder inside the envelope, and label the envelope with the name of the game. (Some of the larger pieces will have to be folded to fit into the folder.) Your new Bible game is now well-protected.

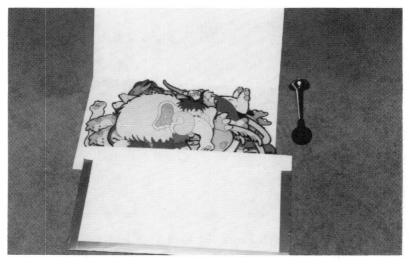

After you play the game, return it immediately to its storage envelope. Games protected in this way will last and last. My Bible games travel all over the country, but they still look new, even after a number of years of being used.

Now let's take a look at some Bible games! Thousands and thousands of kids and teens have played each of the Bible games you are about to see. I trust that you will be able to use some of these games in your ministry. I hope that the kids you minister to will enjoy these games as much as "my kids" have!

# PART TWO

# Twenty Bible Games
# to Make
# Christian Education Fun

Each of the following games has been thoroughly "kid-tested." They have been used with large groups and small, in a number of different states and foreign countries, in all types of teaching situations.

I am presenting them in the way that they have been most effective in our ministry. They work well just as they are given here. However, please feel free to modify any game you find here and make it your own. You may have an idea that will simplify the game, or in some way make it even more exciting for your students. Experiment with these games, and hopefully they will spark some ideas for games of your own!

# Zonk!

This game has been the all-time favorite of kids (and adults) everywhere! I usually use *Zonk!* as the Bible game for the first night of a crusade in a new church, because it is so simple and exciting.

The idea for this game came at a time when I just couldn't seem to come up with any new ideas. I didn't know if the idea would even fly, but it has been very successful. I'm sure your church children will love this game, just as mine have!

Briefly, here's now *Zonk!* is played. The student answering the Bible question correctly comes to the game board and chooses one of 48 brightly-colored felt circles. The teacher turns the circle over for the student, revealing a number on the back. The number, of course, is the number of points scored for that student's team.

When a child is at the board, he may choose as many circles as he wants! But, if a circle is turned over revealing an empty space instead of a number, the student has to stop, and loses all the points from his turn. He has chosen a *Zonk!*

## Making the Game

At a local fabric store, purchase 12 colors of the brightest felt you can find. If you are making the game for the regular board, simply buy 12 of the felt squares that measure approximately 9" x 12". If you are making the game for the giant board, get one-fourth yard of each of 12 colors.

Cut out four circles from each color, 3" for the regular board, or 7" for the giant. This will give you a total of 48 circles in 12 colors.

From an office supply or school supply store, buy the white vinyl stick-on numerals, usually made by Dennison. You will need a total of 36 numerals. Get the 1" size for the regular game, or the 2" size for the giant game.

Stick one numeral in the center of each circle, numbering the circles from 1 to 10. You'll have either three or four of each number. Leave one circle of each color blank, with no number. These are the *Zonks!*

(You'll notice in the photo of my giant *Zonk!* game that each of the circles has a smiley face circle on the front. The only reason for this is that the numbers could be seen through the felt! I had bought cheap felt, and it was too thin! Be sure to purchase a good-quality felt.)

Make a word card saying *Zonk!*, or cut out felt letters spelling *Zonk!*, and your game is finished. You're ready to play it next Sunday!

Be sure to make the storage envelope for the game so that it will be protected the very first time you take it to class.

## Playing the Game

Start with the circles scattered at random across the board. If possible, set the game up before the first students arrive. They will notice the colorful game the moment they walk in the door.

When you are ready to play *Zonk!*, divide your teams, and choose a student as the starter, handing her a horn or bell. The starter can give the signal from her own seat. Select one of the adult helpers as the game spotter, or act as spotter yourself.

Explain the rules. "Today we're going to play a brand-new Bible game! It's called *Zonk!* Boys against the girls! Who's

going to win?!

"Listen closely as I explain the rules. When I ask a question, do not stand until Mike honks the horn. The horn sounds like this." (Pause until Mike honks it.) "Mrs. Evans will be the game spotter. She will choose the first person to stand after the horn sounds. If you stand up before she hears the horn, Mrs. Evans will not call on you.

"When Mrs. Evans calls on you, if you answer the question correctly, you may come up to the game board. Choose one circle by touching it lightly. I will turn the circle over for you. The number on the back of the circle is the number of points you score for your team!

"Now, when you come up here, you may choose as many circles as you want!" (Pause) "But, if I turn one of your circles over, and it is blank on the back, you have chosen a *Zonk!* If you choose a *Zonk!*, you have to stop, and you lose all the points from your turn!

"So, when you come up here, choose a few circles, score

35

some points for your team, but stop before you get a *Zonk!*"

As a child chooses circles from the board, remove them, showing the crowd the points on the back. Add the points in your head, and announce his score after each circle is chosen. He decides after each circle if he wants to stop or continue. Once the child decides to stop, write his score down, or announce it to an adult scorekeeper, who writes it down.

Once a child stops, and her score is written down, the points are there to stay. Another child getting a *Zonk!* later in the game does not erase the points on the score sheet.

For added excitement at the close of the game, have a final question just for the boys, and one just for the girls. The points are doubled on the final two questions.

### Variations and Suggestions

1. As the game *Zonk!* is played and the score is written down, do not announce the total score until the end of the game. This helps build suspense. The students, of course, can add the points in their heads as the game progresses, but very few do.

2. Never mention to any student that one circle from each color is a *Zonk!* Again, very few kids figure that out.

3. You may want to remove a few of the *Zonks!* before you

set the game up, just to reduce the chances of getting a *Zonk!*
I usually pull four *Zonks!* out the first time I play the game
with a new group, just to reduce their chances of getting a *Zonk!*

4. If you choose another method of putting the white
numerals on the felt circles (such as liquid embroidery and
stencils), use numbers from 100 to 1,000 instead of 1 to 10.
Points are cheap, and they make the game exciting!

5. Variation — *Jeopardy Zonk!* Place a sticker or symbol
on the backs of four blank circles. Pull out four of the regular
*Zonks!*, and set them aside. The four circles with the stickers
on the back are *Jeopardy Zonks!* If a child chooses one of the
*Jeopardy Zonks!*, he not only loses his points, but the points
go to the other team!

# Rabbit Hunt

When the idea of *Rabbit Hunt* first began to develop, I had in mind a game for the younger kids (Beginners and Primaries). But at the time we first made the *Rabbit Hunt* game, my wife and I were teaching a class of Junior High young people. One Sunday morning, on impulse, I brought the *Rabbit Hunt* game into the Junior High department and used it.

The students loved it, and begged to play it again the next week! I was amazed, but realized that it was not just a game for the little kids.

The student answering the Bible question correctly comes to the game board and chooses one of 14 bushes. Rabbits are hiding behind many of the bushes. If a gray rabbit is discovered behind a bush, that student scores 1,000 points for his team! A brown rabbit scores 2,000 points, and a white rabbit is worth 3,000 points!

But, if a student finds a bear, his team loses the last rabbit they found! Watch out for the bears!

### Making the Game

Begin by making nine rabbits from poster board: three gray, three brown, and three white. (See pattern, page 171.) You will also make three brown bears using the pattern on page 206. Enlarge these on a plain paper copier to the appropriate size, or draw them on poster board with watercolor markers.

The bears and rabbits need to be laminated to make them durable. Attach Velcro or felt to the backs, depending on the type of fabric on your game board.

These animals should be approximately 3" tall for the regular board, or 8" for the giant board.

Next make 14 bushes from green felt. These do not need to be elaborate. (Notice the bushes in the photo.) Trunks and branches may be drawn in with brown markers. The bushes should be large enough for the rabbits and bears to easily hide behind. If you are using the Herculon board, stitch two small pieces of Velcro to the back of each bush at the top.

Make the two large rabbits from gray poster board for the sides of the game board, laminate them and attach Velcro, and you are ready to play *Rabbit Hunt*!

Don't forget to make your storage envelope!

### Playing the Game

This game must be in place before the students arrive. It is almost impossible to set the game up in front of the students without them seeing what is behind the bushes.

Place the nine rabbits and three bears at random across the board, then place the bushes over the animals, covering

them completely. (Two of the bushes will, of course, be empty.)

When you are ready to play the game, announce your teams, designate an adult to be the game spotter, and give the horn or bell to a student to be the starter.

Explain the rules: "Today we are going to play a Bible game called *Rabbit Hunt*. Who is going to win? Listen carefully as I explain the rules for the game.

"After I ask a question, be sure not to stand until Tina honks the horn. Mr. Perkins is our game spotter today. He will choose the first student to stand after the horn is honked.

"If you answer the question correctly when Mr. Perkins calls on you, you may come to the board and choose a bush. I will take your bush off the board.

"If you find a gray rabbit behind your bush, your team scores 1,000 points! If you find a brown rabbit, you score 2,000 points! If you find a white rabbit, your team gets 3,000 points!

"But, if you find a bear, your team loses the last rabbit you got! Don't get a bear!"

Each student who answers a question is allowed to remove only one bush. To keep score, simply place the rabbits along the bottom of the game board as they are revealed, girls' rabbits on one side, boys' on the other.

In this way, you can easily see which is the last rabbit when a bear is found. The rabbit is removed from the board, and the points are lost. Place the bear in the space vacated by the rabbit. If a team finds a bear on their first turn at the board, place the bear at the bottom of the board, but no points are lost.

At the end of the game, quickly total up the points for each team from their line of rabbits at the bottom of the board, and lead the winning team in a rousing cheer!

### Variations and Suggestions

1. Once or twice at any point during the game, have a slightly more difficult bonus question. If the player answers it correctly, he is then allowed to remove two bushes instead of one. Announce this before you give the question.

2. At the close of the game, you might have a double question just for the girls, and one just for the boys, allowing the students to receive double points, or take two bushes, or both!

Of course, if the points are doubled, then a bear would mean that the last two rabbits would be removed! Point this out when you announce the double points.

# Survival

This has been a popular game, as it also involves animals, and almost all kids love animals. This game can be used successfully with Primaries through Junior High.

A boy answering the Bible question correctly comes to the board and removes one of 20 cactus circles from his team's side of the board. On the back of each cactus circle is one of three animals — a roadrunner, a coyote, or a rattlesnake.

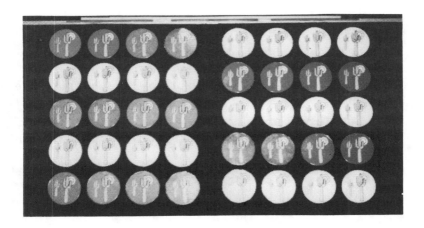

He then chooses a cactus circle from the girls' side of the board, again finding one of the three animals. A rattlesnake wins over a coyote, a coyote wins over a roadrunner, and a roadrunner wins over a rattlesnake.

If the boys' animal is the winner, both circles go to the boys' team for 2,000 points. If the girls' animal wins out, both circles go to the girls for 2,000 points. Either team can get the points from any turn, no matter which team's player is at the board.

### Making the Game

Begin by making 40 circles out of poster board. Make 12 yellow, eight red, 12 purple, and eight sky blue. Or simply choose four colors that are pleasing to you in combination with each other.

The circles should be 3" in diameter for the regular board, or 7½" for the giant board.

Draw the sun and cactus design on the face of each circle with a watercolor marker, or photocopy the designs found on page 172, cut them out, and paste them in place.

Separate the red and yellow circles from the blue and purple, giving you two stacks of 20 circles each. On the back of each of the red and yellow circles, draw or photocopy one of the three animals found on page 172. Make six rattlesnakes, seven coyotes, and seven roadrunners.

On the backs of the blue and purple circles, make six coyotes, seven rattlesnakes, and seven roadrunners. The red and yellow circles are for one team, the blue and purple for the other.

(Note: If you are planning to laminate this game with Contact paper, use watercolor markers rather than permanent

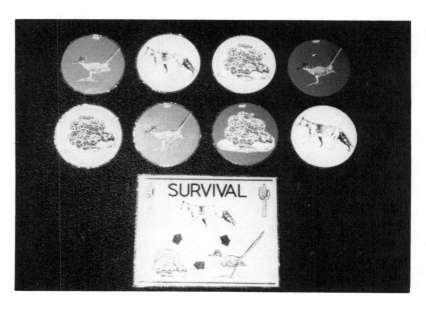

ones. Permanent markers will bleed under the Contact paper lamination.)

Laminate your circles, attach a piece of Velcro to the animal side of each, and make the *Survival* card showing the relationship of each animal to the others. Your *Survival* game is ready to play!

### *Playing the Game*

On the left half of your board, place the blue and purple circles in horizontal rows of four. The top row should be purple, the second row blue, the third row purple, etc. Place the red and yellow circles in similar fashion on the right half of the board, top row yellow, second row red, etc. The cactus design, of course, will be facing out, with the animals on the back.

After choosing a starter, dividing the teams, etc., explain the rules of the game. "Today we are playing a new Bible game called *Survival*. Which team will win? Listen carefully as I explain the rules.

"When you answer a question correctly after the game spotter calls on you, you will come to the board and choose two cactus circles. The red and yellow circles on the right side are

for the girls, the blue and purple circles on the left side are for the boys.

"Let's say that a boy answers the first question. He will come to the board and choose a circle from the boys' side, then one from the girls' side.

"Let's say that he finds a coyote on the boys' side, and a roadrunner on the girls' side. As you know, a coyote can kill a roadrunner, so both circles go to the boys' side for 2,000 points! But, if he finds the roadrunner on the boys' side, and the coyote on the girls' side, both circles go to the girls' side for 2,000 points!"

(Show the *Survival* card.) "A rattlesnake can kill a coyote, a coyote can kill a roadrunner, and, believe it or not, a roadrunner can kill a rattlesnake! No matter who is at the board, either team can get the points!"

No scorekeeper is needed for this game. Keep score right on the board by placing the captured circles in a vertical column in the empty space along the outside edge of the board — boys' points on the left, and girls' points on the right.

If a child chooses two circles with the same animal on both, he chooses two more, one from each side. The team that wins out on this one gets all four circles, or 4,000 points! One little girl got tie after tie on her turn, until she had sixteen circles! The next circles she chose won that turn for the boys, so she gave them 18,000 points! You should have seen the excitement and cheering!

## Variations and Suggestions

1. If you desire to keep the score secret until the end of the game to build suspense, choose an adult scorekeeper, and do not put the captured circles back on the board.

2. As a child chooses circles from the board, hold the first circle she chooses with the animal facing out so the children remember what animal was chosen first.

As the second circle is chosen, hold both circles out, with the boys' circle toward the boys' side of the board, the girls' circle on the other side.

3. Look at the circles twice before you announce the winner on each turn. It is very easy to get confused on a turn, but the children will correct you!

# Matchmaker

Here's a memory game that your students will enjoy playing. It's popular with Primaries through Junior High.

Each child who answers a Bible question comes to the board and chooses two numbered squares from a grid of 20. Behind each square is a brightly colored shape (stars, hearts, etc.). If the child finds two of the same shape, he has made a match, and scores points for his team.

If the child does not make a match, his two squares are put back up, covering the two shapes. The other students try to remember the location of those shapes for future opportunities to score points by making matches.

### Making the Game

Make 20 squares of colored poster board or felt, 10 each of two colors that compliment each other. (My regular game is red and gray; my giant game is light blue and dark lavender.)

The squares should be 4" for the regular board, or 9" for the giant board.

Number the squares from 1 to 20, with the odd numbers all on one color of poster board or felt, the even numbers all on the other color. Use the white Dennison stick-on vinyl numerals available at any office supply store. For the regular game, use 1" numerals; for the giant game, use 2" numerals.

If your squares are made of poster board, laminate them and fasten Velcro on the back, top and bottom.

Using the patterns starting on page 173 make the following shapes from poster board: four blue stars, four yellow triangles, two pink hearts, two orange Xs, two green circles, two purple squares, and two white bonus circles (write the word "BONUS" in black letters). Laminate these shapes, and glue Velcro or felt to the back of each.

Make the title card saying *Matchmaker*. Laminate it and put Velcro or felt on the back. Make your storage envelope, and your *Matchmaker* game is ready to play!

### Playing the Game

Set up the *Matchmaker* game before the children arrive in the classroom. Begin by putting the numbered squares in place on the board in horizontal rows of five. (Locate the center of the board, and center the #3 square at that point. Position the other squares in the first row in relation to the #3 square.)

When all 20 squares are positioned, place one of the poster board shapes behind each square. (Two squares will be empty.)

When it is time to play the Bible game in class, divide your teams, choose your game spotter and starter, and explain the rules.

"We have a brand-new Bible game today! It's called *Matchmaker*! Listen carefully to the rules.

"Each time I ask a Bible question, listen for the signal, and try to be the first one to stand up after you hear it. Miss Simmons will choose the first person to stand after the signal.

"If you answer the question correctly, I will have you come to the game board and choose two squares. Behind each square, you will find a shape — hearts, circles, stars, etc.

"If you find two of the same shape, you have made a match, and a match is worth 1,000 points for your team! If you find two different shapes, you do not score any points, and we will put your squares back up. Everyone else will try to remember what was behind your squares.

"If you find a circle that has the word 'BONUS' on it, you do not need to make a match. A bonus circle is worth 1,000 points by itself! If your team finds both of the bonus circles, that match is worth 3,000 points!

"At the end of the game, the team with the most matches wins the game.

"Before we begin, here is one important rule — when someone is at the board choosing squares, do not call out numbers! If you call out a number, your teammate at the board cannot choose that number! Also, you lose your chance to win the quiet seat prize! So remember, don't call numbers!

"Let's play *Matchmaker!*"

### Variations and Suggestions

1. Keep score right on the board. When a match is made, place the shapes together in the empty spaces at the sides of the board — boys' matches on one side, girls' matches on the other.

2. If the two empty spaces are chosen on the same turn, you may choose to honor that as a match.

3. You may want to make four bonus circles instead of

two. One time, put in all four bonus circles, the next game put in only two or three.

4. On the final question or two, allow the child to pick four squares instead of two. This greatly increases their chances of making a match. Announce this before giving the question.

5. When a match is made and the shapes are placed at the side of the board to score, put the squares back in their original spaces, but place them sideways. This indicates to the children that the square has already been chosen, and is now empty.

6. Be firm about the "no calling out numbers" rule when a student is at the board. If you enforce the rule one time, the children will refrain from calling numbers for the rest of the game.

7. If a child picks one of the two empty spaces (if you are using only two bonus circles), and picks a shape, turn the empty square sideways in its original space, and replace the other square over the shape. The child's turn has ended.

# Dinosaur Daze

Dinosaurs are hot stuff these days! This is a colorful, exciting game that really appeals to kids. When playing *Dinosaur Daze*, a child answering the Bible question correctly will come up and choose a number card that tells him the number of dinosaurs he may choose from the board.

On the back of each dinosaur, the student will find the number of points he scores for his team. If he finds a large "E" on the back of a dinosaur, he has chosen an "Extinct" dinosaur. He has to stop at that point, and loses all the points from his turn. If he finds a "Fossil" dinosaur, he finishes his turn, but the points go to the other team!

The excitement is keen each time a child goes to the board, as the other team hopes for a "Fossil"!

### Making the Game

Using the dinosaur patterns starting on page 176 , trace around the patterns on white poster board and cut out. Then add your own bright colors and details with watercolor markers. Laminate with Contact paper. You may wish to save yourself some time by purchasing an already-made dinosaur bulletin board display from Trend, available at school supply stores. It is called *Fantasaurus*. You will need to purchase two sets. At present, they cost about six dollars a set. This will give you 26 brightly-colored dinosaurs for use on the giant board.

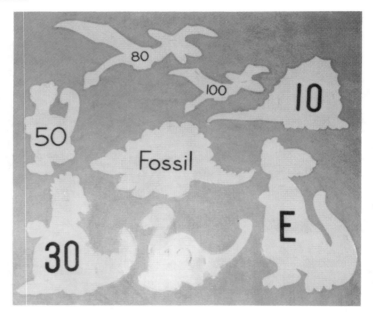

Stencil large numerals on the backs of 21 of the dinosaurs, using numbers ranging from 10 to 100. On four of the remaining dinosaurs, stencil a large capital "E". Stencil the word "Fossil" on the back of the one remaining dinosaur.

Laminate the dinosaurs, and put Velcro on the back of each.

Make 14 number cards from bright yellow poster board. These should be approximately 5" x 7", with 4" numerals. Make three 1s, four 2s, four 3s, and three 4s. Laminate the cards for durability.

*Number cards for* Dinosaur Daze

Make your storage envelope, and you are ready for the excitement of *Dinosaur Daze!*

### Playing the Game

Position the 26 dinosaurs around the game board. Lay the 14 yellow number cards face down on a nearby table or chair. Choose your game starter and spotter, and announce the rules.

"Today we are going to play a really exciting game called *Dinosaur Daze!* This game is going to be fun! Listen carefully as I explain the rules.

"When I ask a Bible question, do not stand up until you hear the signal. Mr. Davis is the spotter today. He will choose the first person to stand after the signal.

"If you answer the question correctly when Mr. Davis calls on you, you may come up and choose a game card. Your game card will tell you how many dinosaurs to choose from the board: one, two, three, or four.

"When you choose each dinosaur, I will take it off the board for you. On the back of each dinosaur is a number, anywhere from 10 to 100. This is the number of points that you score for your team.

"If you find a dinosaur with a large 'E' on the back, that dinosaur is extinct. If you choose a dinosaur that is extinct, you have to stop, and you lose all the points from your turn!

"But wait! It gets worse than that! If you find a Fossil, you finish your turn, but all your points go to the other team! Don't get a Fossil!"

As each child chooses dinosaurs from the board, add the points in your head, and announce their total after each dinosaur chosen. This helps build the excitement, as the other team is hoping for a Fossil. At the end of each student's turn, announce the total to the scorekeeper, who writes it down. A "Fossil" or "Extinct" dinosaur, of course, does not change the scores that are already recorded from previous turns.

### Variations and Suggestions

1. If you will be playing *Dinosaur Daze* repeatedly with the same group of children, they will quickly learn which dinosaur is the "Fossil." To remedy this, make only 19 numbered dinosaurs, and make the two extra dinosaurs as Fossils, giving you a total of three Fossils. Each time you set up the game, leave two Fossils out, changing the Fossil dinosaur each game.

Be sure to make the Fossil dinosaurs from a style of dinosaur that has not already been used for the four "Extinct" dinosaurs.

Another option: Make all 26 dinosaurs with numbers on the back. Then make four "E" decals and one "Fossil" decal that could be taped to the back of any dinosaur, covering the number. In this way any of the 26 dinosaurs can easily become the "Fossil" or the big "E"!

Laminate the decals, just as you did with the dinosaurs.

2. When making the numerals, "Es," and "Fossils" on the backs of the dinosaurs, stencil them, using watercolor markers. (If you use stick-on vinyl numbers, the outline of the number will show through the front when the dinosaur is laminated.)

3. On the last question of the game, or on the final question for each team, set aside the number cards, and let the student choose four dinosaurs. Double the point values on the dinosaurs chosen on this turn. Announce this bonus before you ask the question.

4. Occasionally, for a "high-risk" game, put three Fossils into the game!

5. Never tell the class how many Fossils or Es are in the game.

# Leap Frog

This is a game that we have been using for only about a year, but the response has been tremendous. We have used it with all different ages.

A child answering a question comes to the board and chooses a frog from her side of the board. She tries to get her frog safely across the stream by choosing one log from each of three rows of logs. If one of the logs chosen turns out to be an alligator, the frog dies, and that is the end of the child's turn. If the student gets her frog safely across, she scores 1,000 points for her team.

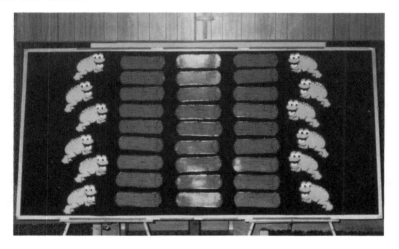

If one of the logs chosen is a "PASS" log, the frog is automatically safely across for 1,000 points, and another frog journey may be attempted on the same turn.

### Making the Game

Make 27 logs from brown poster board, using the pattern on page 184. Photocopy seven of the alligators on green mimeograph paper, and paste them on the backs of seven logs. (Or simply draw the alligators on the backs of seven logs, using a green watercolor marker.)

The logs should be 12" long for the giant 4' x 8' board, or

4½" long for the regular 27" x 36" board.

Write the word "PASS" on the backs of two of the logs. Laminate all 27 logs. Fasten Velcro to the back of each.

If you are using a flannelboard instead of a Velcro board, make the logs of brown felt instead of poster board, and draw the alligators on the backs of seven logs with green markers. Write "PASS" on the backs of two logs with a black marker.

Make 12 frogs from green poster board, six facing left, six facing right. (See pattern on page 185.) The frogs should be 10" long for the giant board, or 4" long for the regular board. Laminate the frogs and fasten Velcro on the back. (If using a flannelboard, make the frogs from green felt.)

Make your storage envelope, and you are ready to play *Leap Frog!*

### Playing the Game

Arrange all 27 logs in three vertical rows in the center of your game board. Place six frogs in a vertical row on each side of the board, facing the center of the board.

(The frogs should be positioned fairly close to the rows of logs, so that there is an empty space at both sides of the board.)

Divide teams, choose your adult game spotter and a child game starter, and explain the rules of the game.

"Today, class, we are playing a Bible game called *Leap Frog!* The boys are against the girls! Which team will win?

"Here are the rules. If you answer a question correctly after the game spotter calls on you, you may come to the board and choose a frog from your side of the board. This row of frogs is the girls', and this row is the boys'.

"After you have chosen your frog, you will choose a log from the row of logs nearest your frog. I will turn the log over for you. Then you will choose a log from the center row, which I will turn over for you. Finally, you will choose a log from the last row.

"If your frog makes it safely across the stream in those three hops, he scores 1,000 points for your team! But it's not as easy as it looks! You see, some of these ' logs ' are not logs at all! They are alligators! Do you know what happens to your frog if he lands on an alligator? If your frog lands on an alligator, he gets eaten, and that is the end of your frog, and the end of your turn! Don't land on an alligator!

"Now if you land on a log that says ' PASS, ' your frog is automatically safely across the stream. You may then choose a second frog, and try to get him across the stream on the same turn!

"Remember, don't stand up until you hear the signal after each question, and watch out for alligators!"

## *Variations and Suggestions*

1. To keep score, take each frog that successfully makes the journey across the stream and place it on the side of the board toward which the frog was heading. At the end of the game, simply count frogs.

2. Turn each log over as the child chooses it, announcing "safe," "alligator!," or "pass," rather than waiting until all three logs have been chosen for the child's turn.

3. I put a small mark (that blends in with the design) on the face of each log that has an alligator. In this way, I can tell in advance when a child has chosen an alligator, or is "safe."

4. Just for fun, you may want to put name tags on the frogs, giving six frogs girls' names, the other six boys' names. You may even want to name the alligators!

# Double Dip

This is an ice cream game, and what kid doesn't like ice cream? Like *Leap Frog*, we have only used *Double Dip* for about a year, but it has been a popular game.

The student answering the Bible question correctly comes to the board and chooses one of 12 ice cream cones. Directly below his cone is a limit card, which will be turned over at the end of his turn.

The student may then choose as many as four scoops of ice cream, placing them one at a time on his cone. Point values on the back of each scoop are revealed as they are chosen.

When the student stops choosing scoops of ice cream, his points are totaled, and his limit card is revealed. If he has stopped below the limit, he keeps his points. If he has gone over the limit, he loses all his points!

No one knows, of course, what the player's limit is until after he has chosen to stop. If a player stops right on the limit, he receives a bonus circle worth extra points.

### Making the Game

Make 12 ice cream cones from brown poster board. (See

the pattern on page 185.) The cones should be 9" tall for the giant board, or 4" tall for the regular board.

Now, using the patterns on page 186, make 30 scoops of ice cream, in various colors representing various flavors. You may use colored poster board or white poster board that has been painted. The scoops should be approximately 5½" tall for the giant board, or 2" tall for the regular board. Stencil the point values on the back of each scoop: 5, 10, 15, 20, and 25.

Make 12 limit cards from white poster board, 5" x 7" for the giant board, or 2" x 2½" for the regular board. On the back of each limit card, stencil the following numerals: 20, 25, 30, 35, 40, 50, 55, 60, 70, and one more each of 25, 30, and 70. Use 3" numerals for the giant board or 1" for the regular board.

Make four circles out of fluorescent orange poster board, and stencil the word "BONUS" across the face of each. The circles should be 5½" for the giant game, 2" for the regular game.

Laminate all the game pieces, glue Velcro on the back, and make your storage envelope. You now have another exciting Bible game, ready for your students to play!

### Playing the Game

This game takes a couple of minutes to set up, so you probably will want to have it on the board before class starts. (See photo for suggested arrangement.)

Explain the game to your students. "We have a new Bible game called *Double Dip*! It's an ice cream game! How many of you like ice cream?

"Listen carefully as I explain how the game is played. When you answer a question correctly, you may come to the board and pick one of the ice cream cones. The white card below your cone is called your limit card.

"After you have chosen your cone, you may choose some scoops of ice cream to put on it. You may choose one, two, three, or four scoops. We won't let you put more than four scoops on your cone because it could get kind of messy.

"On the back of each scoop of ice cream is a number: 5, 10, 15, 20, or 25. Five is the lowest; 25 is the highest. As you choose your scoops, I will announce your points, and you decide when to stop.

"Let's say that a boy comes up here and chooses this cone. This card below the cone will be his limit card. Let's say that he chooses three scoops of ice cream, and stops with 45 points. After he decides to stop, I will turn his limit card over. If his limit is 45 or higher, he keeps all his points. If his limit card says 40 or lower, he loses all his points!

"The limit cards go from 20 to 70. The lowest card is 20, the highest card is 70. Don't go over the limit! If you stop right on the limit, you get one of the bonus circles, worth 50 extra points! Let's play *Double Dip!*"

As each child chooses scoops of ice cream, stack them in place on his cone, announcing his point total each time. If the child goes over the limit, remove his cone and scoops, announcing that there are no points on this turn.

If the child stops below the limit, leave his cone and scoops on the board, and announce his score to the scorekeeper. If he stops right on the limit, place a bonus circle on top of his stacked cone, and announce his score to the scorekeeper, including his 50-point bonus.

### *Variations and Suggestions*

1. At the conclusion of the game, you may want to have a double question or two. The points on the scoops are doubled, the limit cards are doubled, even the bonus circles are doubled. Announce this before you give the question, and make sure that the kids understand that the limit cards now range from 40 to 140.

2. Do not reveal the limit card until the student has decided to stop.

3. The student must stop with four scoops, even if his point total is low.

# Sea Monster

This is a game that has been a hit with the kids! I played it in a Crusade with a crowd of 330 kids recently, and the response was tremendous.

The student answering the Bible question comes to the board and chooses a number card telling her how many fish she may choose from the board (1, 2, or 3).

She then chooses that many fish. On the back of each fish is the number of points that student has scored for her team (from 100 to 1,000). If the student finds a shark, she stops choosing fish, and loses all the points from her turn! If she finds a sea monster, she finishes her turn, but her points go to the other team!

When a student is at the board, the other team is always hoping for a sea monster!

### Making the Game

Make 12 number cards from yellow poster board, 5" x 7". Number these with 4" numerals: four 1s, four 2s, and four 3s. Laminate these cards.

Using the fish patterns starting on page 187, make 20 fish from brightly-colored poster board. Use a black watercolor marker to fill in the eyes, gills, fins, and other details.

On the backs of 16 of the fish, stencil numerals from 100 to 1,000. On the backs of three of the fish, stencil the word "SHARK!" On the back of the one remaining fish, stencil "SEA MONSTER!"

Laminate the fish, fasten Velcro on the backs, and your *Sea Monster* Bible game is ready to play! Be sure to make your storage envelope.

### Playing the Game

Place all 20 fish on your game board, and spread the 12 number cards face-down on a nearby table or chair.

Select your game spotter and starter, announce your teams, and explain the rules.

"When I ask a Bible question, do not stand until you hear the signal given by our game starter. Mr. Wells is the spotter today; he will choose the first person to stand after the signal. When Mr. Wells chooses you, if you answer the question correctly, you may come to the board to play *Sea Monster*.

"You will start by choosing a number card, which will tell you how many fish you may take — one, two, or three. You may then select that many fish from the board. On the back of each fish is a number — 100, 500, 700, maybe even 1,000! These are the points you score for your team.

"But, if you find a shark, you have to stop choosing fish, and you lose all the points from your turn! But it can be even worse than that! If you find a sea monster, you finish your turn, but your points go to the other team! Don't get a sea monster!"

As the student chooses each fish, announce her points to the class. At the end of her turn, announce the total points to the scorekeeper to be recorded for her team.

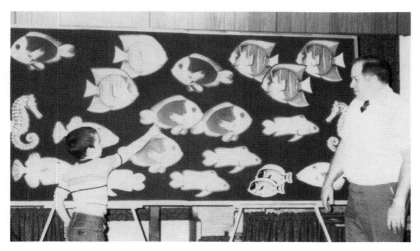

### Variations and Suggestions

1. Do not tell the students how many sharks or sea monsters there are in the game.

2. If you play the game more than once with the same group of children, they will quickly learn which fish is the "sea monster." Buy or make more than 20 fish, and make several "sea monsters." Each time you play the game, put a different fish in as the "sea monster."

3. On occasion, play the game with several "sea monsters" in the game!

4. On the last question or two, set aside the number cards, let the children pick three fish, and double the points on every fish! Announce this before you ask the question.

# Sky War

In this Bible game, your students will engage in an aerial dogfight, doing their best to knock out "enemy" planes before their own planes are shot down. It's the pink Air Force against the blue Air Force!

The child answering the Bible question correctly comes forward and chooses a game card. His card is turned over, revealing "pink," "blue," "cloud," or "choose." If his card says "pink" or "blue," the child takes that color plane off the board, "shooting it down." If the card says "cloud," the student takes down one cloud, as well as the plane behind it. If he picks a "choose" card, he may "shoot down" an enemy plane or a cloud.

There are enemy planes hidden in the clouds. To win the game, a team must not only shoot down the four enemy planes visible on the board, but also the two enemy planes hidden in the clouds. This, of course, involves the danger of shooting down one's own planes by mistake!

### Making the Game

Make 16 game cards from white poster board. These should be 5" x 7". On the backs of four of these, color a 4" circle with a bright pink marker. Color a blue circle on the backs of four other cards. Use watercolor markers. Stencil the word "Cloud" on the backs of four cards, and the word "Choose" on

71

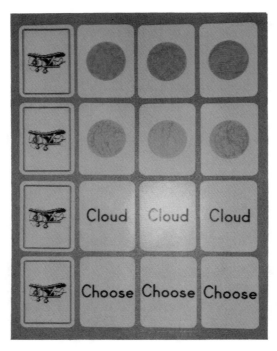

the remaining four. Laminate these game cards.

Make six clouds from white poster board, using the pattern on page 191. These should be 18" to 20" long for the giant board, or 8" long for the regular board. Glue Velcro to the outer edges of the back of each cloud. This is so when the clouds are removed during the game, the planes hidden behind them will stay on the board and won't stick to the clouds.

If you are using a flannelboard rather than a Velcro board, you may make the clouds from white felt. Be sure that the felt is thick enough so that the color of the planes does not show through.

Make six planes from light blue poster board, and six planes from pink poster board. These should be 16" long for the giant board, or 6" long for the regular board. Laminate the planes, and glue Velcro or flannel on the back of each. (See patterns on pages 189 and 190.)

Make the *Sky War* title card, laminate it, and put Velcro

on the back. Make your storage envelope, and *Sky War* is ready to play!

## Playing the Game

This game should be set up on the board before the students arrive, if possible, so that you can hide the planes behind the clouds.

Position the six clouds on the board, hiding two blue planes and two pink planes, and leaving two clouds empty. Place the remaining eight planes on the board. Set the 16 game cards face down on a nearby table or chair.

Choose your game spotter and starter, and give the rules for *Sky War*.

"Today we are playing a Bible game called *Sky War*! Your team needs to shoot down the enemy planes before they shoot your planes down! The blue planes are the boys' planes; the pink planes are the girls'.

"If you answer the Bible question correctly, you will come to the front, and choose a game card. If you find a pink dot, you shoot down a pink plane; if you find a blue dot, you shoot down a blue plane, even if it is your own plane! The first team to shoot down all six of the other team's planes is the winner.

"You probably noticed that there are only four planes for each team showing. There are planes hiding in the clouds! You need to locate and shoot down the two enemy planes in the clouds.

"If you choose a card that says 'cloud' on it, you may choose a cloud, and shoot down the plane behind it. But, be careful not to shoot down your own plane!

"If your game card says 'choose,' you may shoot down an enemy plane or a cloud. Let's play the game!"

As each student chooses a card, allow her to remove the appropriate plane or cloud from the board. If one team has shot down the two enemy planes behind the clouds, and gets a "cloud" card, they still must shoot down another cloud, as well as any plane behind it.

73

### Variations and Suggestions

1. Vary the number of planes behind the clouds from two (one blue, one pink) to six (three blue, three pink). Of course, be sure to place an equal number from each team behind the clouds.

2. On the last question or two, have a double question. This may be done in one of two ways. First, the student chooses two cards, and removes the two appropriate planes or clouds. The second way is for the student to select only one card, which is doubled — two pink planes, two clouds, or whatever. Announce doubles before you give the question.

3. The game may be played without the game cards on occasion, with the students choosing enemy planes or clouds on each turn.

# The Lost Dutchman

This Bible game involves a treasure hunt for a legendary gold mine, lost for almost a hundred years! Excitement will build as your students get close to finding the mine. Rattle-snakes, old maps, and the thrill of finding gold all add to the fun.

As each student answers a Bible question, he or she is allowed to come to the board and choose one of 12 prospector cards. Each team is trying to acquire three items to enable them to head for the mountains and find the mine: a map, a lantern, and a pick.

When either team has found the three required items on the back of the prospector cards, they are allowed on the next turn to begin searching the mountains for the mine. The team finding the gold mine wins the game and the gold!

### Making the Game

Make 12 prospector cards from blue poster board, 7" x 10" for the giant board, or 2½" x 3½" for the regular board. On the backs of three of the cards, draw or photocopy the map. (See patterns starting on page 192.) Make lanterns on the backs of three cards, and picks on the backs of three cards.

One prospector card should read "Lost in desert! Lose your map!" Another should say, "Stepped on rattlesnake! Lose a turn!" (See patterns on page 196.)

The last prospector card should show the map, lantern, and pick, and should read, "Choose one!"

Make seven cactus plants from green poster board, ranging in size from 4" to 11" for the giant board, smaller for the regular board. (See patterns on pages 192 and 193.)

Make six mountains from brown poster board. (In the photo, the largest mountain is 21" long.) For the regular board, the mountains would be 8" and smaller. (See pages 194-195.)

On the back of each mountain, stencil one of the following — "GOLD MINE" (with drawing of the mine), "Getting close!," "Read the map again!," "Keep looking!," "Sorry!," and "Better luck next time!"

Make the title board for the game, laminate each of the game pieces and put Velcro on the back, and your *Lost Dutchman* Bible game is ready! (Remember to make your storage envelope.)

### Playing the Game

Place the 12 prospector cards in a straight row across the bottom of the board. Position the six mountains across the top two-thirds of the board, and place the title card at the very top. Scatter the cacti among the mountains.

Choose your game starter and spotter, and announce the rules for *The Lost Dutchman.*

"Today we will be playing a Bible game called *The Lost Dutchman.* We will be looking for a gold mine that has been lost for a hundred years! The team finding the mine wins the game.

"Listen as I tell you the true story behind the game. Way back in the late 1800s, an old Dutchman named Jacob Walsh would come into Phoenix, Arizona, with bags of gold. People would ask Jacob where he got the gold, and he would tell them that he had his own gold mine.

"East of Phoenix are some strange-looking mountains called the Superstition Mountains. That's where Jacob Walsh lived, in those mountains. People would follow him home to the mountains, hoping to find his mine, but no one ever did.

"Jacob died without ever telling anyone where his gold mine was located. People have been looking for it ever since. Hundreds of people have died searching in the desert for the mine, but the location of it still remains a mystery.

"We're going to try to find that mine today! Listen carefully as I explain the rules.

"When you correctly answer a Bible question, you may come to the board and choose a prospector card. On the back of your card, you will find one of three things: a map, a pick, or a lantern. Your team needs one of each of those items so you can head for the mountains and find the mine.

"When your team has the map, lantern, and pick, you may start checking the mountains. One of the mountains has the gold mine! The team finding the gold mine wins the game!"

As each child chooses a card, place the cards facing out on an easel or chair. Place the boys' items on one side, the girls' items on the other. In this way, the teams can easily see what items they have, and which items they still need.

When a child finds the "Choose One!" card, allow that

child to name that card as a lantern, pick, or map. The card then becomes that item for his team. (The card may not be changed to another item later in the game.)

When a child finds the rattlesnake card, his team loses a turn, meaning that the next question goes automatically to the other team.

If a student finds the "Lost in desert! Lose your map!" card, her team loses their map, and must find another. If her team has not yet acquired a map, they do not forfeit their map when they do find one.

When either team has acquired all three items, they may start choosing mountains on the next turn. Only one mountain, of course, is chosen on each turn.

The team finding *The Lost Dutchman* gold mine wins the game!

## Variations and Suggestions

1. If you play the game a number of times with the same group of children, they will quickly learn which mountain is the gold mine. To avoid this, do one of two things: make two or three extra gold mine mountains, and place only one in the game each time, or make a gold mine sticker that can be removed easily and transferred from one mountain to another. Be sure to place the gold mine in a different spot each time you play the game.

2. If one team finds more than one pick, map, or lantern, do not place the extra items on the easel or chair with that team's items. Lay the extra items to the side. These cards may be shuffled in with the other prospector cards if needed. (Example: One team may find all three lanterns on their first three turns. The two extra lanterns may be shuffled in with the other cards and placed back on the board, giving the other team a chance for a lantern.)

3. If one team has found two maps, then gets the "Lose your map" card, they only lose one map. They do not need to find another map.

4. On the last question or two, allow the student to double

his chances and choose two prospector cards or two mountains. Announce this before giving the question.

# Magic Squares

Magic Squares has been quite popular with the Primary and Junior classes, and we have used it on occasion with the Beginners.

The student answering the Bible question correctly comes to the board and chooses one of 16 felt squares. When his square is removed, a colored circle is revealed. The circle is then placed to one side of the board.

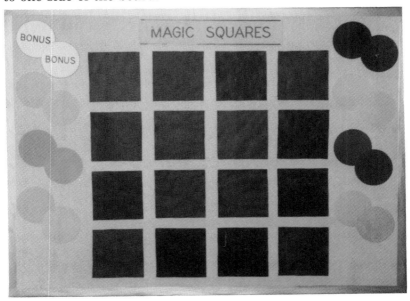

As the game progresses, both teams' circles are placed on their respective sides of the board. Some circles will match others in color. Each match scores 1,000 points for the team.

At the end of the game, any circles not matching are simply removed, scoring no points.

### Making the Game

Make eight squares of each of two colors of felt, for a total of 16 felt squares. Choose two colors that compliment each other. (The game pictured uses red and purple squares.) The squares should be 9" for the giant board, or 4½" for the regular board.

If you are using a Velcro board, it is best to stitch two small pieces of Velcro to the top two corners of each square to make sure that they will stay in place on the board. The squares could also be made of poster board, laminated, with Velcro or flannel on the back.

Make 16 circles from poster board. The circles should be 7½" in diameter for the giant board, or 3½" for the regular board. Make four yellow, two blue, two green, two pink, two orange, two black, and two white with the word "BONUS" stenciled on them. Laminate the circles, and fasten Velcro or flannel on the back of each.

Make your *Magic Squares* title card from poster board. Laminate it and put Velcro or flannel on the back. Make your storage envelope, and *Magic Squares* is ready for your class to play!

### Playing the Game

*Magic Squares* must be set up before the students arrive, or at least out of their sight. It is impossible to set it up in front of the students without them seeing the circles.

Place the 16 circles on the board in four horizontal rows. Arrange the 16 felt squares in rows in such a way that they completely cover the circles. Put your title card in place, choose your game spotter and starter, and explain the rules.

"We have a new Bible game today called *Magic Squares*! Listen as I give the rules.

"On the board are 16 squares. If you answer a Bible question correctly, I will have you come to the board and choose a square. Behind each square you will find a circle. The circles are of many different colors.

"We will place the boys' circles on this side of the board, and the girls' circles on that side. When you find a circle that matches the color of another of your team's circles, you have made a match worth 1,000 points!

"If you find a circle that says 'BONUS' on it, that circle is worth 1,000 points by itself! It doesn't need a match to score! If your team finds both of the bonus circles, that match is worth 3,000 points!

"Let's play *Magic Squares!*"

As the students remove squares, place their circles on the appropriate side of the board. Set the felt squares aside, rather than putting them back on the board.

If a team ends up with three of the yellow circles, it counts only as a single match. If one team finds all four, it counts as two matches.

As the game progresses and matches are made, announce the totals each time a new match is made.

### Variations and Suggestions

1. No adult scorekeeper is needed for this game, as the score is kept right on the game board.

2. On occasion, you may want to leave out two circles of one color, leaving two empty squares. The team choosing either

of these gets no points on that turn.

3. Have double and even triple questions. Allow the students to remove two squares on a double, and three squares on a triple. Example: A 10-question game would allow you six single questions, two double questions, and two triple questions, to remove all 16 squares. Announce doubles and triples in advance of the question.

4. On occasion, you may want to play the game with as many as three or four bonus circles. It is best to play with only two most of the time.

5. When making the game, you may want to fasten the colored circles directly to the backs of the squares. This would allow you to set the game up in front of the children without them seeing the circles. When playing the game, you would turn the square over and set it to the side of the board, with the circle showing.

For instance, if your squares are made of felt, glue colored felt circles to the backs of the squares. Either side would adhere to the flannelboard. Stencil the word "Bonus" on the two white circles with permanent marker or liquid embroidery.

# Clown Toss

This game, and the one to follow, are the only games in this book that are not original with us. *Clown Toss* is a carnival-type game, available from U.S. Toy Company. The game is ready-made; just set it up in class and use it.

At this writing, *Clown Toss* costs $12.50. My old *Clown Toss* game had traveled all over the country, but it lasted about 10 years.

You may request a catalog or order *Clown Toss* from: U.S. Toy Company, Inc., 1227 East 119th Street, Grandview, Missouri 64030-1117 (1-800-255-6124).

When playing *Clown Toss*, the student answering the Bible question correctly comes to the front of the room and is given four Styrofoam balls to throw. He or she attempts to knock down three little clowns that are sitting on a ledge. Each clown knocked off the ledge scores 1,000 points for that team.

This game is popular with Primaries through Junior Highers.

### Making the Game

The beauty of this game is that it is ready-made for you. If you have been wanting a new game for Sunday School or Junior Church, but just haven't had the time to make one lately, perhaps this game is for you.

In fact, several of the other carnival-type games in the U.S. Toy catalog are suitable for use as Bible games. The games on the board are usually more effective, but the carnival-type game can be a nice change of pace for your class.

### Playing the Game

Set up *Clown Toss* on a table, desk, or chair, following the instructions included in the game. Choose a game spotter and starter, and explain the game to your students.

"Today we are going to play a brand-new Bible game called *Clown Toss!* Listen carefully as I give the rules for the game.

"As I ask each Bible question, Jennifer will honk the horn. Be careful not to stand until you hear the horn. If Mr. Lewis chooses you as the first person to stand after the horn, you will have the chance to answer the question and play *Clown Toss.*

"You will stand behind the tape line on the floor, and I will give you four of these Styrofoam balls to throw. The object is to knock the clowns down off their little ledge. Any clown that you knock down scores 1,000 points for your team!

"If you knock a clown partway off the ledge, but he doesn't fall, you don't score any points for your team, unless, of course, you can knock him all the way off with another shot.

"Let's play *Clown Toss!*"

## *Variations and Suggestions*

1. On the last question or two, have bonus questions. The child either gets extra throws, or the score on each clown is doubled. Announce bonus points before giving the Bible question.

2. As a *general* rule (there are exceptions), the boys will probably throw more accurately than the girls. This is true for almost any age group, and is the result of a combination of factors, including their physical make-up or simply the fact that they've often had more practice. To make the competition more fair, consider using coed teams with an equal number of boys and girls.

3. Before you play the game for the first time, have a few of your "early birds" test the game for you. As they try the game, determine how far the throwing line should be from the game. This will vary with different age groups. Put a piece of masking tape on the floor for the throwing line.

(Note: The Styrofoam balls are very light, and it is more difficult to knock a clown down than you would think.)

4. After your class has played the game a couple of times, they will discover that it is easiest to knock the clowns down by hitting them at the bottom, flipping them forward.

When your class discovers this, announce a new twist the next time you play the game. Any clown that falls forward is worth 1,000 points; any clown that falls backwards is worth 2,000 points! Most kids will try for the 2,000 points.

5. If you play the game with older students (Juniors or Junior Highers), they will often throw the balls hard enough to dent them. When the original balls are worn out, go to any craft store for cheap replacements.

6. The *Clown Toss* game comes with only three balls, but it is usually best if you give the students four throws.

# Good Guys and Bad Guys

The idea for this game came from a friend of mine who directs a large children's ministry. I spoke for him at a junior retreat, and he saw our *Zonk!* game. He took the *Zonk!* idea and developed it into a new game, *Good Guys and Bad Guys.* I took his idea for the game and revamped it. This is the version I am presenting here.

A child answering the Bible question correctly comes to the game board and chooses one of 40 cowboys. On the back of each cowboy circle is a reward poster, telling how much reward money that cowboy's capture is worth. That amount of money is given to the child in play money.

The child at the board may take as many cowboys as he wants to. At any time, the child may stop, take his money to one of two banks (two student volunteers, one from each team), and his turn is over. If the player picks a cowboy circle with a big, white hat on the back, his turn is over, and he loses all the money from his turn. He captured a good guy!

One of the cowboys turns out to be the sheriff, resulting in money being transferred from one team to the other.

At the end of the game, the team with the most money deposited in its bank wins the game.

### Making the Game

Make five circles from each of eight colors of poster board for a total of 40 circles. The circles should be 7½" in diameter for the giant board, or 3" in diameter for the regular board.

Using the pattern on page 197, draw or photocopy the cowboy on the face of each circle. On the backs of nine circles, draw or photocopy the white hat. Make the sheriff's star on the back of one circle, and draw or photocopy the reward posters (patterns on pages 197 and 198) for the remaining 30 circles.

Make the reward posters in the following values: five each of $50, $100, $200, and $500, three $400 posters, and two $750 posters. Laminate the circles, and fasten Velcro or flannel on the back of each.

Photocopy the play money on pages 198-199 on green paper. You will need ten 50s, twenty-five 100s, ten 500s, and ten 1,000s. Cut to size on a paper cutter. The money is more realistic if it is not laminated.

Make your storage envelope, and you are ready to play *Good Guys and Bad Guys!*

## Playing the Game

Arrange the 40 cowboy circles in five horizontal rows across the board. The reward posters and white hats, of course, are hidden on the backs. Place the reward money in a stack to the side of your board. Choose a boy and girl to be the bankers for each team.

Choose a spotter and game starter, and announce the rules for the game.

"Today we are going to play a really exciting Bible game called *Good Guys and Bad Guys!* I'm sure you'll enjoy it! Listen carefully as I give the rules.

"If you are the first person to stand after the horn sounds, and you answer the Bible question correctly, you may come to the board and choose a cowboy. On the back of each cowboy is a reward poster, telling how much money you get for capturing that cowboy. I will give you that much reward money for your team.

"When you come to the board, you may choose as many cowboys as you want! But if I turn one of your cowboys over, and there is a big, white hat on the back instead of a reward poster, you have captured a good guy! If you get a good guy, that is the end of your turn, and you lose all the money from your turn. Don't get a good guy!

"One of the cowboys is really the sheriff. If you find the sheriff circle, you become the sheriff for the rest of the game! When someone from the other team is at the board and has a lot of money, before they get a good guy or say 'stop,' you may say, 'You're under arrest!' You may then take their money to your bank, and their turn is over! But, if you are the sheriff, you may only arrest one person from the other team during the entire game.

"When you are at the board, and you decide to stop, you take your money to the bank and deposit it. This is the First National Boys' Bank, and this is the First National Girls' Bank.

Once your money is in the bank, of course, it is safe for the rest of the game. At the end of the game, the team with the most money in the bank wins the game! Let's play *Good Guys and Bad Guys!*"

## *Variations and Suggestions*

1. As with the other Bible games, have a bonus question or two at the end of the game. On bonus questions, double the reward money for each cowboy chosen! Announce the bonus feature before you give the question.

2. If you play the game with the same group every week, they will quickly discover which color circle has the sheriff. To avoid this, make several sheriffs on different colored poster board circles, and put only one sheriff in the game each time. Or, make a removable sheriff sticker, and place it on a different cowboy for each game.

3. When using a heat laminator, the outline of the reward posters is sometimes visible through the front of the poster board circles. Laminate a circle or two, and if the shapes are visible from the front, laminate the circles with clear Contact paper instead.

4. Give the reward money to the student immediately after each cowboy is chosen. If a good guy is chosen, the student hands all his or her money back to you.

5. At the conclusion of the game, have an adult quickly count all the money in the banks and announce the total deposits.

6. As with the other Bible games, it is usually best if the teacher, rather than the student, removes the circles from the board.

7. When the student who finds the sheriff circle finishes his turn, have him sit in the front row, where he is ready to arrest a member of the other team. The student finding the sheriff circle does not lose the sheriff privilege if he finishes his turn by finding a good guy.

# The Green Machine

The idea for this game came to me during a game of Ping-Pong in my garage. A friend from church and I were playing, and he slammed the ball, hard. The ball arched over my head, and I turned around just in time to see it disappear behind a sheet of plywood leaning against the garage wall. I heard the ball ricochet several times very rapidly between the two studs in the wall.

I moved the sheet of plywood and retrieved the ball, but what I had just seen stuck in my mind. We stopped playing Ping-Pong and made *The Green Machine*.

A student answering a Bible question correctly is given three Ping-Pong balls to drop into a hole at the top of *The Green Machine*. As each ball drops, it ricochets back and forth off small pegs or nails in the game. When the ball reaches the bottom, it lands in a numbered slot, showing the points it has scored.

If two of the balls land in the same numbered slot, those two are dropped again by the student, adding more points to the score. Double scores and the red dot feature add extra excitement to the game.

This game has been used successfully with every age group.

### Making the Game

You will need a piece of ¼" plywood that measures 19" x 24." Cut four 1 x 4s, two 24" long, the other two 17½" long. Nail or screw these together to form a rectangular frame measuring 19" x 24". Nail this frame to the plywood back to form a shallow box. (See diagram on page 200.)

Paint the inside of this box flat black, and paint the edges and outside of the box the brightest green you can find.

Cut a piece of 3/16" Plexiglas to a 19" x 21" rectangle. This will be the face of *The Green Machine.*

Drill a 1½" hole in the top piece of the frame. This hole should be centered. As the game is played, the kids will drop the Ping-Pong balls through this hole. If a Ping-Pong ball does not fit through the hole easily, sand the hole until it is large enough.

Inside the box, drive finishing nails into the plywood back. These nails should be placed in horizontal rows, evenly spaced.

The rows should be 2½" from each other. The first row will be placed 2" from the top inside of the box, the next row 4½", the third row 7", etc.

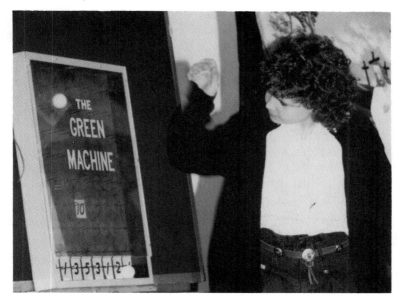

Place the nails in each row 2" apart. The top row will have nine nails, with the end nails ¾" from the inside of the frame of the box. The second row will have eight nails, with the end nails 1¾" from the frame. The third row will have nine nails, lined up directly below the nails in the top row. The fourth row will have eight, which line up directly below the nails in the second row. If you stagger the rows of nails in this way, the ball will bounce from row to row, instead of passing straight through.

This will give you eight rows of staggered nails, with the last row 3" from the bottom. Place a ninth row of nails 1½" from the eighth, with each nail lined up directly below the nail in the eighth row. This will form spaces at the bottom of the game into which the balls will drop and remain.

Glue number cards to the back of the game in each of these spaces. Make these from yellow poster board. Number them in the following order: —1, 2, 1, 3, 5, 3, 1, 2, and —1.

Place an extra nail ¾" above the sixth row of nails. This extra nail should be centered between the fourth and fifth nails in the row. This forms an extra stopping point for the ball. It is difficult to get the ball to stop there, so label it 10 points.

Screw the sheet of Plexiglas to the front of the frame. It should be flush with the top of the box, leaving a 3" opening along the bottom of the game to retrieve the Ping Pong balls.

Purchase 2" vinyl stick-on letters at an office supply store, spelling out "THE GREEN MACHINE." Separate the letters from the backing, and place them on a sheet of waxed paper. Paint the letters with the same green paint that you used to paint the outside of the game. When the paint has dried, trim any excess paint, and arrange the letters carefully to spell out "THE GREEN MACHINE."

Purchase three white Ping-Pong balls, and color a large red dot on one of the balls with a red felt-tip marker.

Make a storage box from cardboard, or a protective cloth cover, and you're in business!

### Playing the Game

Place *The Green Machine* on an easel, music stand, or chair so that it leans back at a slight angle. Choose your game spotter and scorekeeper, and a student to be the game starter. Explain the rules for the game.

"Today we are playing a brand-new Bible game — *The Green Machine*! Listen as I explain the rules.

"If you are the first student to stand after the signal, and you answer the question correctly, you will be allowed to come up here to play *The Green Machine*. I will give you three Ping-Pong balls, which you will drop into *The Green Machine* — like this." (Demonstrate by dropping the balls, one by one. Let each ball reach the bottom before you release the next one.)

"When each ball reaches the bottom, it tells you your score. If two of the balls go into the same slot, you keep that score, and drop the balls again, adding some more points to your score! (This rule does not apply if two go into the minus 1 slot.)

"Let's play *The Green Machine!*"

As each child drops the Ping-Pong balls, have them stand to the side of the game, so the other children may see. When a ball stays in the 10 position, cover the hole so the child will have to pause and announce, "Lisa just got a 10! Unless, of course, she knocks it down! Don't knock it down!" The other team, of course, will call, "Knock it down! Knock it down!"

When two balls go into the same scoring slot, hand them back to the student, and have her drop them again, adding to her score. Leave the third ball where it landed. If two go into the same slot again, or one goes into the slot where the third ball already is, they are dropped the third time.

Announce the child's score after each ball lands. If a 10 is knocked down, it becomes a lower score. Subtract the appropriate number of points.

### Variations and Suggestions

1. Occasionally, as in the other Bible games, have bonus questions where the points are doubled. Announce the bonus before you give the question.

2. On the last few questions of a game, play the red dot feature. You may not want to use this the first few times you use *The Green Machine*, and then, when you do use it, it will be something new.

Color a large, red dot on one of the Ping-Pong balls. Drop all three balls into a grab bag (or a lunch sack). Have each student playing the game remove the balls one at a time. If the red dot ball is chosen first, the entire score for that turn is tripled! If the red dot is chosen second, the score is doubled! If the red dot comes out last, it is a regular score on that turn.

For a really exciting finale, have a double question for each team. Everything is doubled on these final two questions. Red dot chosen first equals six times the score! Red dot out second equals four times the score! Red dot out last, the score is still doubled.

Of course, on any bonus question, the minus 1 slot is

also multiplied, and becomes a minus 2, minus 4, or whatever.

3. Play Pink and Blue. Cut pink index cards to fit in four of the scoring slots, and blue cards to fit in four. Make the center scoring slot half pink, half blue.

As a child drops each of the balls, he chooses what the score for that ball will be — 1,000; 2,000; 3,000; 4,000; or 5,000; or minus 1,000; 2,000; or 3,000. If the ball lands in a blue slot the score goes to the boys (or is subtracted from the boys); if it lands in pink, it goes to the girls (or is subtracted from the girls). If it lands in the center slot (pink and blue), it goes to the team of the child making the drop.

The student has five chances out of nine that the points will go to his team. He may, of course, choose the minus points, hoping that the ball will land in the other team's slot, subtracting from their score.

# Green Machine Baseball

This game utilizes *The Green Machine* described in the last section. If you have not yet made your *Green Machine*, see page 94.

To play *Green Machine Baseball*, a child drops a single Ping-Pong ball into *The Green Machine*. A ball scoring 1, 2, or 3 signifies a single, double, or triple. A 5 or 10 means a home run. Minus 1 gives the batter an out.

The questions alternate between the two teams. If a member of the opposing team is on a base to which the batter is to go, the batter advances to the next base ahead of his opponent.

Runs are tallied on the scoreboard, and the team with the most runs wins, as in regular baseball.

### *Making the Game*

If you already have *The Green Machine*, most of the work is done! Simply make four bases out of white cardboard or canvas, cut to 14" square. Number these bases 1, 2, 3, and H. Make a scoreboard, or draw one on your marker board, and you are ready for *Green Machine Baseball*!

### Playing the Game

Set your *Green Machine* on an easel or music stand, and place just one Ping-Pong ball in it. If you desire, make the baseball "stitching" on the Ping-Pong ball with a red felt-tip marker.

Lay your bases on the floor in a small diamond. Choose your "umpire" (the adult game spotter), and a child for game starter. Explain the rules for *Green Machine Baseball*.

"We are going to play a new game with *The Green Machine*, called *Green Machine Baseball*! Which team is going to win? Listen closely as I explain the rules.

"The first Bible question will go to the boys; the second will go to the girls. The questions will alternate between the two teams for the entire game.

"If you answer the question correctly, you will come up to 'bat.' You will drop one Ping-Pong ball into *The Green Machine*. If your ball lands in the 1 slot, you get a single, so you go to first base. A 2 means a double, and a 3 gives you a triple. If you score a 5 or a 10, you get a home run! A minus 1 gives you an out!

"If someone from the other team is on the base that you are supposed to go to, you go to the next open base. Let's say that a boy gets a single, but there is a girl on first, and a girl on second. The boy would go to third base!

"If one of your team members is on base, he or she will always move one base ahead of you. If you get a triple, and someone from your team is on base, you would go to third, and your team member would go home for a run!

"At the end of the game, the team with the most runs wins the game. Let's play ball! Batter up!"

## Variations and Suggestions

1. Always be sure to have an even number of questions, so that both teams get an equal number of times "at bat."

2. All runs are force only. For instance, if there is a girl on second, and another girl gets a double, the girl on second would go to third, not home.

3. At the end of the game, any runners remaining on base simply return to their seats and do not score.

4. On the final question for each team, you may wish to have a bonus question. Any runs crossing the plate on the bonus questions are doubled, scoring two points each! Announce bonus points before giving the question.

5. Three outs for one team would, of course, end the game. Give the other team one final turn "at bat," even if the two teams have had an equal number of questions.

6. If the bases are loaded by the members of one team, any "hit" by the other team is a home run, since they would automatically go home!

# Bible Treasure

This Bible game is different from all the others in the book, in that it is not played by teams, and no one wins or loses. In *Bible Treasure*, it is every child for him or herself.

The student answering the Bible question correctly comes to the game board, and chooses one of 14 brightly colored circles. The teacher takes the circle from the board. If a treasure chest is found behind the circle, the student gets a prize from a grab bag or treasure chest.

Although this game is not played by teams, you will be amazed at the way the students will cheer when another student finds a treasure chest.

*Bible Treasure* has been very popular with Beginners, Primaries and Juniors.

### Making the Game

Make 14 circles from seven colors of felt, two circles of each color. The circles should be 12" in diameter for the giant board, or 5" for the regular board. If you are using a Velcro board, it is best to stitch two pieces of Velcro at the top of each circle to make sure that they will adhere to the board properly.

Make eight treasure chests from brown poster board from the pattern on page 200. The treasure chests should be 9" long for the giant board, or 3½" long for the regular board. Laminate and put Velcro on the back.

Make nine "Sorry" cards from white poster board, the same size and shape as the treasure chests (see page 201). Fasten Velcro to the back of each.

You may use the parrot, flag, and sword patterns on page 201 to add a pirate motif to the game if you wish.

Make a title card and storage envelope, and your *Bible Treasure* game is finished!

### Playing the Game

Before the students enter your classroom, set up the *Bible Treasure* game. This game is difficult to set up in the presence of the children without them seeing what is behind the circles.

Put your title card in place at the top of the board, then arrange five of the treasure chests and the nine "Sorry" cards at different spots around the board. Place the 14 felt circles on

the board, being sure to cover each of the treasure chests and "Sorry" cards. Put two of the remaining treasure chests in the top corners of the board, and the last one in the center of the board at the bottom. Arrange your swords, parrots, and flags on the board.

Choose a game starter and spotter, and give the rules for the *Bible Treasure* game.

"Today we are going to play a game called *Bible Treasure*! We will not have teams for this game; you're all on your own! We're looking for buried pirate treasure!

"When you answer a Bible question, you will be allowed to come to the board and pick one of these colored circles. I will take the circle from the board for you. If we find a treasure chest like one of these behind your circle, you win a prize from the treasure chest! (Or a candy bar, pack of gum, whatever.)

"If you do not find a treasure chest, we will ask another question, and someone else will try. Let's play *Bible Treasure*!"

### Variations and Suggestions

1. As with the other Bible games, have occasional bonus questions, where the child chooses two circles on one turn. Announce the bonus before you give the question.

2. Vary the number of treasure chests hidden behind the circles. If the students learn that there are always five treasure chests hidden, when the fifth one is found, the game is over for them. Put six in one game, only three or four in the next game.

3. If you have a small group of students (14 or less), be sure that each child has at least one turn at the board.

4. When playing the *Bible Treasure* game with Beginners, you may wish to have a small consolation prize for those who do not find a treasure chest. (This can save you from irate parents in the hallway after class — "Well, why didn't my child get a prize?")

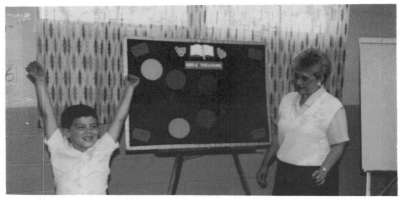

5. It is usually best to use several of the other Bible games first, then introduce *Bible Treasure*. If you play *Bible Treasure* as your very first Bible game, the children will expect prizes for the other games as well.

# Busy Bees

*Busy Bees* is a Bible game for the younger students. It has been popular with Beginners and Primaries.

The child answering the Bible question correctly comes to the board and chooses a honeybee, taking it from a flower and putting it on the beehive that belongs to his team. At the end of the game, the team with the most honeybees on their hive wins the game.

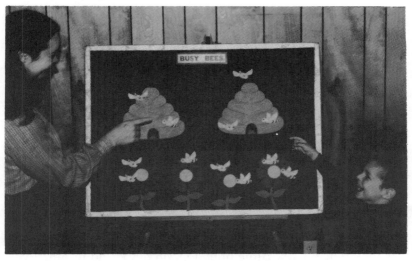

This game is very simple, but has been a favorite with the very young.

### Making the Game

Make 12 honeybees from yellow felt, poster board, or construction paper, using the patterns on page 202. Six bees should be facing right, six facing left. The bees should be approximately 3½" long for the regular game, or 9" long for the giant game.

Laminate the bees if you desire, and put Velcro or flannel on the back of each. (If your bees are made of felt, they will not need to be laminated.)

Make two large beehives from tan felt, using the pattern on page 203 as a guide. The hives should be 10½" wide for the regular game, or 25" wide for the giant game. (The giant hives will have to fold in half to fit your storage envelope.)

Using the pattern on page 202, make two flowers from red felt, with yellow centers and green leaves and stems. Make two identical blue flowers. The heads of the flowers should be 5½" in diameter for the regular board, or 16" for the giant board. (You will have to fold the giant flowers in half as well to fit in the envelope.)

If using the Velcro board, stitch Velcro on the backs of the hives and flowers to make sure that they will adhere to the board properly. Make your "Busy Bees" title card and the storage envelope, and your new game is ready to play!

### Playing the Game

Place your title card at the top of the game board, and put the two hives in the center of the board, with some space between them. Place the four flowers along the bottom edge of the board, and put all 12 bees on the flowers.

Choose your game starter and spotter, and explain the rules to the children.

"We are going to play a new Bible game today! It's called *Busy Bees*! Listen carefully to the rules.

"When I ask a Bible question, do not stand up until you hear the signal. If you are the first person to stand after the signal, Mrs. Wilson will call on you, and you may answer the question. Do not answer the question until she calls on you.

"When you answer the question correctly, you may come to the board and choose a honeybee. You may take your bee off the flower and put it on your beehive. This hive is for the girls, and this hive is for the boys.

"At the end of the game, the team with the most honeybees on their hive will win the game. Ready? Let's play *Busy Bees!*"

## *Variations and Suggestions*

1. As with other Bible games, have bonus questions. The child answering the question is allowed to take two bees and put them on the hive.

2. Play the game in reverse, with six bees starting on each beehive. The object of the game is to get all your worker bees to the flowers first.

3. Mark one, two, or three bees with the word "prize" on the back. The child choosing that bee gets a small prize in addition to helping his team win the game. Use this feature only occasionally.

4. With very young children, do not even divide the class into teams. No team competition is needed. Simply allow the children to move the bees to the flowers, or vice versa, when they have answered a question. Try to make sure that every child gets a chance.

5. Place only one beehive on the board, with all 12 bees on or around it. Place the flowers at the bottom of the board as usual. The boys place bees on the blue flowers; the girls place them on the red flowers. The team with the most honeybees on their flowers wins the game.

# Build-A-Bug

This is a very simple game. It was actually designed for the younger classes, but even the Juniors have responded enthusiastically to it.

The two teams compete to see who can assemble their own ladybug first. Each time a child answers a Bible question, he or she is allowed to come to the board and add a piece to his or her team's bug.

*Build-A-Bug* is very easily made, and has been a lot of fun!

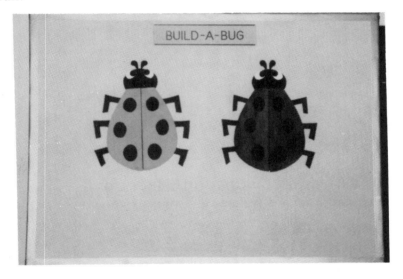

### Making the Game

If you are using the small board, you will need five 9" x 12" squares of felt: two black, one orange, one red, and one white. (If you are using the larger board, you may have to use felt off a bolt.) From black felt, make two bug bodies, complete with legs. (See pattern on pages 203-205.) The bug bodies should be 8½" tall for the regular board, or 21" tall for the giant board. (The giant bug bodies will have to fold to fit in the storage envelope, but the felt folds easily.)

Make two wings from red felt, and two wings from orange felt. Add black spots with permanent marker or pieces of black felt.

Make two heads from black felt, and four antennae from black felt. Make four eyes from white felt, adding details with black permanent marker.

Make the *Build-A-Bug* title card for the game, put together the storage envelope, and your game is ready to play!

### Playing the Game

Place the two bug bodies near the center of the board, with a little space between them. Place the orange wings on one side of the board, and the red wings on the other side. Put the head, eyes, and antennae from one ladybug on one side of the board, and the parts from the other bug on the other side of the board.

Put your title card in place at the top of the board, choose the game spotter and game starter, and explain the rules.

"We are going to play a brand-new Bible game called *Build-A-Bug!* The first team to put its ladybug together wins the game! Listen as I explain the rules.

"Each time I ask a Bible question, Mark will ring the signal bell. If you know the answer to the Bible question, stand up after you hear the bell. Miss Winslow will decide who is the first person to stand. Don't stand up until you hear the bell!

"When you answer the question correctly, you may come to the board and add one part to your bug. The head goes on first, then your team may add any of the other parts on each turn. If you finish building your ladybug before the other team finishes, your team wins! Let's play *Build-A-Bug*!"

### *Variations and Suggestions*

1. Each team has its bug body when the game starts. They do not need to answer a question to get the body.

2. Allow the children to position the body parts as they choose them. (You may want to help them straighten the first wing as it is put on.)

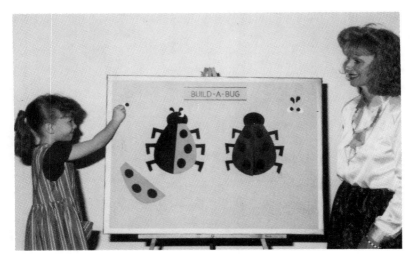

3. Have bonus questions where the child puts two parts on in one turn. Announce the bonus before you give the question.

4. For the older students, add number cards to the game. Make 12 cards from poster board, 5" x 7". Write the numeral "1" on five of the cards, and put the numeral "2" on another

five. Write "Remove 1" on the two remaining cards.

Place the cards face down on a nearby table or chair. Each student takes a card before going to the board, and adds one or two body parts to his own bug. The student picking a "Remove 1" card removes a body part from the other team's ladybug, and places it to the side of the board, where it was originally.

5. Most of the Bible games in this book look their best and brightest on a black flannelboard or Velcro board. *Build-A-Bug*, however, looks best on a light-colored board, such as sky-blue.

# Hungry Bears

The final two games in this book were developed by my wife, Janice, for use with Beginners (four- and five-year-olds). These Bible games are very, very simple, but the little ones love them.

Children love animals, and the *Hungry Bears* game and *Chasing Butterflies* game both involve animals. Give these Bible games a try. Your Beginners will love them!

When playing *Hungry Bears*, the child answering the Bible question comes to the board and chooses one of 15 brightly colored bears. The bear chosen is removed from the board. If a yellow fish is found behind the bear, the child receives a small prize. If the child finds a purple fish, she receives a larger prize.

### Making the Game

Make 15 bears from brightly colored poster board or construction paper, following the pattern on page 206. If using construction paper, remember that it fades and loses its color after a time. You may want to simply photocopy the bears on white paper and color them with bright markers.

The bears should be 6½" tall for the regular board, or 15" tall for the giant board. Laminate the bears if you wish, and put Velcro or flannel on the back.

Make 10 fish, six yellow and four purple. The fish should be 3" long for the regular board, or 8" long for the giant board. Laminate the fish, and put Velcro on the back of each.

Make the *Hungry Bears* title card for the game, and make your storage envelope. Your new *Hungry Bears* Bible game is ready to play!

### *Playing the Game*

Position the 15 bears around the game board. Hide three of the purple fish and five of the yellow fish behind eight of the bears. This will leave seven bears with nothing behind them. Place the title card at the top of the game board.

Choose your game spotter and a child to be game starter. When working with Beginners, if you have 15 children or less in your class, you may choose to not even use a spotter and starter. Simply ask the Bible questions, then choose a child to answer and come to the board. Be sure that each child gets an opportunity to answer at least one question.

Announce the rules for the *Hungry Bears* game. "Today, boys and girls, we are going to play an exciting Bible game called *Hungry Bears*! Listen carefully as I give the rules for the game.

"I will ask some Bible questions. These questions are from the lesson today. If you know the answer to one of the questions, raise your hand, and I will call on you. Do not answer the question until I call on you.

"If you answer the question correctly, you may come to the game board and choose a *Hungry Bear*. I will take your bear off the board. If we find a yellow fish behind your bear, you will receive a prize. If we find a purple fish, you will receive an even nicer prize.

"Ready? Let's play *Hungry Bears!*"

## Variations and Suggestions

1. You may choose to make 15 fish, 10 yellow and five purple, so that there is a fish behind every bear.

2. If your students are mature enough to understand team competition, divide into teams, and play *Hungry Bears* for points instead of prizes. A yellow fish is worth 1,000 points and a purple fish is worth 2,000 points.

3. You may want to vary the number of fish hidden behind the bears from game to game.

4. As with other Bible games in this book, have bonus questions. The child chooses two bears on a bonus question. Bonus questions are usually most effective at the conclusion of the game. Announce the bonus before you give the question.

# Chasing Butterflies

This Bible game, like *Hungry Bears*, was developed by my wife for classes of four- and five-year-olds. This is a very simple, colorful game, and the younger children love it.

Children usually associate butterflies with springtime and outdoor fun. They will enjoy this butterfly game.

The child who answers the Bible question comes to the game board and chooses a flower. When the flower is removed from the board, if a yellow butterfly is found, the child receives a small gift. If a blue butterfly is revealed, a larger gift is given.

### Making the Game

Make 18 flowers from brightly colored felt. Make the center of each flower from a contrasting color of felt. The flowers should be 4" in diameter for the regular board, or 10" in diameter for the giant board.

Make eight butterflies from yellow construction paper, and four butterflies from blue construction paper. The patterns for the flowers and butterflies are found on pages 205-207. You may want to simply photocopy the butterflies on white paper and

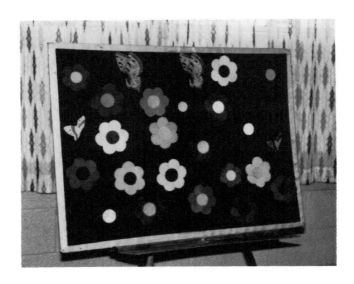

color them with permanent markers. If you plan to laminate the butterflies with Contact paper, use water color markers, as the permanent markers will bleed under the Contact paper.

Glue Velcro or flannel to the back of each butterfly. Make a *Chasing Butterflies* title card for the game, and make the storage envelope. Your game is ready to play!

### Playing the Game

Scatter the flowers across the game board, hiding nine or 10 of the butterflies behind them. You may want to use a game spotter and game starter, having the children stand or raise their hands after a given signal, or you may want to simply ask the questions, giving each child a turn to answer at least one question.

Announce the rules for *Chasing Butterflies.* "Today, boys and girls, we are going to play a new Bible game! It's called *Chasing Butterflies!* Listen as I explain the rules.

"I will ask some questions from the Bible. These questions are from our Bible lesson today. If you know the answer to the question, raise your hand. When I call on you, you may answer the question. Please do not answer the question until I call on you.

"When I call on you, if you answer the question correctly, you may come to the board and choose a flower. If we find a yellow butterfly behind your flower, you will receive a small gift. If we find a blue butterfly, you will receive a larger gift.

"Ready? Let's play *Chasing Butterflies!*"

## Variations and Suggestions

1. You may wish to make 18 butterflies, 13 yellow and five blue, so that there is a butterfly behind every flower.

2. If your students are old enough to appreciate team competition, divide into teams and play the game for points instead of prizes. A yellow butterfly scores 1,000 points, a blue one scores 2,000 points.

3. You may wish to vary the number of butterflies hidden from game to game.

4. Use bonus questions. On a bonus question, the child picks two flowers instead of one. Before you read the questions, remember to announce to your group that these are bonus questions to heighten the excitement.

## PART THREE

# *Sample Questions From the Bible*

To give you an idea of the type of questions we've used, following are 20 sample sets of questions from the Bible: 10 from the Old Testament and 10 from the New Testament. You will notice these questions are all grouped according to themes. This is what we prefer, but we recognize there may be some circumstances, such as at a Christian camp, where it is better to use general questions (e.g. What is the name of the first book in the New Testament?) rather than the theme questions.

You may use or adapt these sample questions to suit your purposes, or you may write your own questions based on your Sunday school lesson so the Bible game can serve as a fun way to review. If you write your own questions, remember to target them to the age group you will be working with. The questions you would ask five-year-olds and 10-year-olds will vastly differ!

A benefit of the Bible games is that any set of Bible questions will work with any of the games, meaning you can rotate your games to keep the interest level high. No matter what Bible story you happen to be studying, you'll have an exciting game on hand to keep your group of children learning and having fun.

# Theme: The Fall *(Genesis 3)*

**1.** Q: How did the earth come into existence?

   A: *God created it.*

**2.** Q: What special creation did God make on the sixth day?

   A: *People.*

**3.** Q: What did God do on the seventh day?

   A: *He rested.*

**4.** Q: What were the names of the first man and woman?

   A: *Adam and Eve.*

**5.** Q: What was the name of the garden where God placed them?

   A: *Garden of Eden.*

**6.** Q: What was the name of the tree that God commanded Adam and Eve not to eat from?

   A: *Tree of knowledge of good and evil.*

**7.** Q: Why did God tell them not to eat from that tree?

   A: *To test their love for him.*

**8.** Q: Who tempted Eve to eat from the tree?

   A: *The devil, in the form of a serpent.*

**9.** Q: What did Eve do, and what did Adam do?

   A: *They both disobeyed God and ate from the tree.*

**10.** Q: What was the result?

A. *They were driven from the garden, and later, death would come.*

**11.** Q: What are the results of their sin today?

A: *Disease, death, war, crime, unhappiness.*

**12.** Q: What was the promise of Genesis 3:15?

A: *God would send a Savior.*

# Theme: Abraham Sacrifices Isaac *(Genesis 22)*

**1.** Q: Give the names of the man and woman in the Bible story today.

A: *Abraham, Sarah.*

**2.** Q: What was the special promise that God made to Abraham?

A: *He and Sarah would have a son.*

**3.** Q: How old were Abraham and Sarah when their son was born?

A: *Abraham — 100 years old, Sarah — 90.*

**4.** Q: What did Abraham name his son?

A: *Isaac.*

**5.** Q: What difficult thing did God ask Abraham to do?

A: *Offer his son Isaac as a sacrifice.*

**6.** Q: Why did God ask Abraham to do this?

A: *To test Abraham's love for God.*

**7.** Q: Does God ever ask us to do things that are difficult?

A: *Sometimes, but he also promises to help us do them.*

**8.** Q: Did Abraham obey God?

A: *Yes.*

**9.** Q: What happened?

A: *Abraham prepared to offer Isaac on top of Mount Moriah, but God stopped him. A ram was offered instead of Isaac.*

**10.** Q: Was it fair for God to ask Abraham to give his son?

A: *Yes, because God gave his Son, Jesus, to die for us.*

**11.** Q: What does God ask us to give to him today?

A: *Our lives.*

**12.** Q: What did the test prove about Abraham?

A: *He loved God.*

# Theme: The Fall of Jericho *(Joshua 2, 6)*

**1.** Q: How many spies did Moses send into Canaan?

A: *Twelve.*

**2.** Q: What was the report that they brought?

A: *"The land is good, but we are not able to overcome the inhabitants."*

**3.** Q: Why didn't the people of Israel go up immediately into the land that God had promised to them?

A: *They didn't believe God.*

**4.** Q: How many spies did Joshua send into Jericho?

A: *Two.*

**5.** Q: Who hid the spies from the king's soldiers?

A: *Rahab.*

**6.** Q: What token (sign) did the spies ask Rahab to put in her window when Israel attacked the city?

A: *The scarlet cord.*

**7.** Q: How did Israel attack the city?

A: *They simply marched one time around the city each day for six days, and seven times on the seventh day.*

**8.** Q: What happened?

A: *God brought the walls of Jericho crashing down, and Israel had the victory.*

**9.** Q: Who won the battle for Israel?

A: *God.*

**10.** Q: What kept Israel from entering the Promised Land forty years earlier?

A: *Unbelief.*

**11.** Q: What brings victory for us today?

A: *Faith.*

**12.** Q: Quote Joshua 1:9.

A: *"Have not I commanded thee? Be strong, and of a good courage; be not afraid, neither be thou dismayed: for the Lord thy God is with thee whithersoever thou goest."*

**13.** Q: Name some times when it is hard for you to trust God.

**14.** Q: Why can we always trust God?

A: *Because he has promised to always be with us.*

# Theme: The World's Strongest Man *(Judges 13-16)*

**1.** Q: What did the angel of the Lord promise to the wife of Manoah?

A: *That she would have a son.*

**2.** Q: What was the son's name?

A: *Samson.*

**3.** Q: How was Samson to be different from other children?

A: *He was to be a Nazarite. His hair was never to be cut, he was never to drink wine, and he was never to touch a dead body.*

**4.** Q: When Samson grew up, what was he famous for?

A: *His tremendous strength.*

**5.** Q: Name two times when Samson used his great strength.

A: *He pulled up the gates of a city and carried them to the top of a hill; he killed a lion with his bare hands; he killed a thousand Philistines by himself.*

**6.** Q: Who was Samson's girlfriend?

A: *Delilah.*

**7.** Q: Why did she want to find out the secret of Samson's great strength?

A: *The lords of the Philistines had promised her money.*

**8.** Q: What three lies did Samson tell her as to how he could be captured?

A: *"Tie me with seven green withs (bowstrings). Tie me with new ropes. Weave my hair into seven locks."*

132

**9.** Q: What was the true secret of Samson's strength?

A: *His hair had never been cut.*

**10.** Q: What did Delilah do when he told her the secret?

A: *She had a barber cut off his hair while he was asleep.*

**11.** Q: What happened to Samson?

A: *He lost his strength and was captured by the Philistines, who put out his eyes.*

**12.** Q: What was Samson's long hair a symbol of?

A: *His dedication to God.*

# Theme: A Boy Does a Man's Job *(I Samuel 17)*

**1.** Q: Who was the king of Israel?

A: *Saul.*

**2.** Q: What enemy nation was encamped against Israel?

A: *The Philistines.*

**3.** Q: Why were the men of Israel afraid?

A: *They were afraid of the giant, Goliath.*

**4.** Q: How tall was Goliath?

A: *Over nine feet.*

**5.** Q: Why wouldn't Israel's soldiers fight Goliath?

A: *They weren't trusting God.*

**6.** Q: Who volunteered to fight the giant?

A: *David, a young shepherd boy.*

**7.** Q: What weapons did David take to the battlefield?

A: *A sling and five smooth stones.*

**8.** Q: Why did David go, since he was not a soldier?

A: *He knew that he could trust God.*

**9.** Q: What happened in the battle with Goliath?

A: *With God's help, David killed the giant soldier, using only a sling.*

**10.** Q: Can we trust God today?

A: *Yes.*

**11.** Q: Do you ever have problems that are too big for you?

**12.** Q: What should you do if you have problems you cannot handle?

   A: *Take them to God.*

# Theme: David Forgives Saul *(I Samuel 18-26)*

**1.** Q: Who was the first king of Israel?

A: *Saul.*

**2.** Q: Whom did God choose as the next king?

A: *David.*

**3.** Q: Why did God choose a new king?

A: *Saul had disobeyed.*

**4.** Q: How did Saul respond to David?

A: *He tried to kill him on several occasions.*

**5.** Q: What should we do when someone treats us as an enemy?

A: *We should treat them with kindness.*

**6.** Q: When did David get his first chance to get even with Saul?

A: *When Saul came into the cave at Engedi.*

**7.** Q: What did David do?

A: *He refused to kill Saul, but merely cut off a piece of Saul's robe as a lesson to the king.*

**8.** Q: When did David have his second chance to get even with Saul?

A: *When Saul was camped with his men in the wilderness.*

**9.** Q: What did he do?

A: *He refused to kill Saul, but took his spear and cruse of water, and later returned them.*

**10.** Q: Why is it hard to forgive others?

A: *They often do mean or unkind things to us.*

**11.** Q: What did Jesus tell us to do in the Sermon on the Mount?

A: *Love your enemies. Bless those who curse you. Do good to those who hate you. Pray for those who despitefully use you.*

**12.** Q: Why should we forgive others?

A: *Because God forgives us.*

# Theme: Naaman Gets Well *(II Kings 5)*

**1.** Q: What was the name of the captain of the Syrian army?

A: *Naaman.*

**2.** Q: What was Naaman's problem?

A: *He had leprosy.*

**3.** Q: The Bible sometimes compares leprosy to what?

A: *Sin.*

**4.** Q: Who told Naaman's wife about the prophet of God?

A: *A little servant girl, brought as a captive from Israel.*

**5.** Q: What did the king of Syria do when he heard about a possible cure in Israel?

A: *He sent Naaman with a letter of introduction and a large reward.*

**6.** Q: Who was the prophet of God?

A: *Elisha.*

**7.** Q: What did Elisha do when Naaman came to his house?

A: *He sent his servant out with the message for Naaman to dip seven times in the Jordan River.*

**8.** Q: How did Naaman respond to the message?

A: *He went away angry.*

**9.** Q: What did Naaman do after his servants talked to him?

A: *He went down and dipped seven times in the Jordan River.*

**10.** Q: What happened?

A: *Naaman's leprosy was cured; his skin was restored.*

**11.** Q: What would have happened if Naaman had refused to do what God said?

A: *He would have died a leper.*

**12.** Q: What does the story of Naaman show us about salvation?

A: *We have to come to salvation God's way, through faith in Christ.*

# Theme: A New Queen *(Esther 1-10)*

**1.** Q:  Why did King Ahasuerus decide to choose a new queen?

   A:  *Queen Vashti had disobeyed.*

**2.** Q:  Who was chosen as the new queen?

   A:  *Esther.*

**3.** Q:  What was the name of Esther's cousin, who had taken care of her when her parents had died?

   A:  *Mordecai.*

**4.** Q:  Of what nationality/religion were Mordecai and Esther?

   A:  *They were Jewish.*

**5.** Q:  How did Mordecai offend Haman, who was ruler over all of the princes of the kingdom?

   A:  *Mordecai refused to bow to Haman.*

**6.** Q:  How did Haman plan to get revenge on Mordecai?

   A:  *He planned to have all the Jews killed, as he knew that Mordecai was Jewish.*

**7.** Q:  To whom did Mordecai turn for help?

   A:  *Queen Esther.*

**8.** Q:  What did Esther do?

   A:  *She invited Haman and King Ahasuerus to two banquets. At the second banquet, she revealed Haman's plan to kill the Jews, which were her people.*

**9.** Q:  How did King Ahasuerus respond when he heard of Haman's plot?

A: *He was angry.*

**10.** Q: What did he do?

A: *He ordered that Haman be hanged, and that the Jews would be allowed to defend themselves.*

**11.** Q: Why do you think Esther became queen?

A: *God had planned it that way.*

**12.** Q: What was the final result?

A: *Esther was able to save her people.*

# Theme: Daniel in the Lions' Den *(Daniel 6)*

**1.** Q: What was the name of the land where Daniel and his friends were taken captive?

A: *Babylon.*

**2.** Q: How did God bless Daniel for his faithfulness?

A: *God exalted him to be ruler of the land, just under the king.*

**3.** Q: Why were the other presidents and princes jealous of Daniel?

A: *Because of his position and his favor with the king.*

**4.** Q: When they tried to find fault with Daniel's life, what evil did they find?

A: *Nothing.*

**5.** Q: What law did the presidents and princes ask King Darius to sign?

A: *No one could ask a petition of anyone, God or man, for 30 days, except if they asked the king.*

**6.** Q: What was the penalty for breaking the new law?

A: *The offender would be cast into a den of lions.*

**7.** Q: What did Daniel do when he learned of the new law?

A: *He continued to pray three times a day, just as before.*

**8.** Q: What happened?

A: *Daniel was thrown into the den of lions.*

**9.** Q: Was Daniel killed?

*A:* *No, because God sent a angel to shut the lions' mouths.*

**10.** Q: What was the final result?

    *A:* *Daniel's accusers were thrown to the lions and killed, and King Darius glorified Daniel's God.*

**11.** Q: Why is it often difficult to do what's right?

    *A:* *Because others often try to lead us astray, or will laugh at us for doing right.*

**12.** Q: What promise of God should we remember when faced with a difficult decision, as Daniel was?

    *A:* *"I will never leave thee, nor forsake thee."* (Hebrews 13:5)

# Theme: Jonah and the Whale *(Jonah 1-4)*

**1.** Q: Why did God want to send a prophet to Nineveh?

A: *No one had ever warned the Ninevites about God's judgment.*

**2.** Q: Whom did God choose to go to Nineveh?

A: *Jonah.*

**3.** Q: What did Jonah do when God sent him to Nineveh?

A: *He got on a ship going in the opposite direction.*

**4.** Q: Have you ever disobeyed God?

A: *Yes, we all have. That is what God calls sin.*

**5.** Q: Why do you think Jonah did not want to go to Nineveh?

A: *The Ninevites were very cruel people; they were the enemies of the Israelites.*

**6.** Q: What did God do when Jonah ran away?

A: *He sent a storm at sea, which threatened the ship and the lives of the men on board.*

**7.** Q: What did the sailors do that caused the storm to stop?

A: *They threw Jonah overboard.*

**8.** Q: Why did Jonah not drown?

A: *God prepared a great fish to swallow him.*

**9.** Q: How long was Jonah inside the fish?

A: *Three days and nights.*

**10.** Q: What happened when the fish spit Jonah out on dry land?

    A: *He went and preached at Nineveh. The entire city repented.*

**11.** Q: Why should we be concerned about others?

    A: *Some have never heard the Gospel.*

**12.** Q: Why is it always best to obey God?

    A: *He knows what's best for us. When we obey, we are in a position for him to bless us.*

**13.** Q: What would have happened to the people of Nineveh if Jonah had not gone?

    A: *The city would have been destroyed.*

# Theme: The Birth of Jesus *(Matthew 1 and 2, Luke 2)*

**1.** Q: Finish the verse: "Thou shalt call his name _____,
for he shall save his people from their _____."
(Matthew 1:21)

   A: *Jesus, sins.*

**2.** Q: Who was the mother of Jesus?

   A: *Mary.*

**3.** Q: In what town was Jesus born?

   A: *Bethlehem.*

**4.** Q: Why was Jesus laid in a manger?

   A: *Because there was no room for them in the inn.*

**5.** Q: Why did Jesus come to earth?

   A: *To save his people from their sins.*

**6.** Q: Who brought the message of Jesus' birth to the shepherds?

   A: *Angels.*

**7.** Q: What did the shepherds do when they heard the message?

   A: *They went to see Jesus.*

**8.** Q: What does the name "Jesus" mean?

   A: *Savior.*

**9.** Q: What other group of people heard of the birth of the new king?

   A: *The wise men.*

**10.** Q:  How did they find Jesus?

A: *They followed a special star.*

**11.** Q:  What gifts did the wise men present to Jesus?

A: *Gold, frankincense, and myrrh.*

**12.** Q:  What was so special about the baby?

A: *He was God's Son.*

**13.** Q:  What did Jesus do to save us from our sins?

A: *He died for us on Calvary.*

# Theme: The Tax Man *(Luke 19)*

**1.** Q: What city did Jesus visit in this Bible story?

A: *Jericho.*

**2.** Q: Name the man at Jericho who was determined to see Jesus.

A: *Zaccheus.*

**3.** Q: Name two things that you know about Zaccheus.

A: *He was a publican, or tax collector. He was short. He was rich. He was dishonest.*

**4.** Q: When Jesus came to Jericho, why couldn't Zaccheus see him?

A: *Zaccheus was "little of stature," and there was a big crowd.*

**5.** Q: What did Zaccheus do in order to see Jesus?

A: *He climbed a sycamore tree.*

**6.** Q: What did Jesus do when he saw Zaccheus in the tree?

A: *He asked Zaccheus to come down so he could go to his house.*

**7.** Q: Did Jesus know who Zaccheus was?

A: *Yes. He called Zaccheus by name, and he knew all about him.*

**8.** Q: If Jesus knew that Zaccheus was dishonest, why did he go to his house?

A: *Jesus came to save sinners. He loves everyone.*

**9.** Q: What happened to Zaccheus when Jesus came to his house?

A: *He received the Lord as his Savior.*

**10.** Q: What did Zaccheus do that showed that he was sincere in receiving Jesus?

A: *He promised Jesus that he would pay the people four times the amount he had cheated them, and he would give half of his money to the poor.*

**11.** Q: Quote Luke 19:10 by memory.

A: *"For the Son of man is come to seek and to save that which was lost."*

**12.** Q: What did the crowd do when they saw that Jesus had gone to the house of Zaccheus?

A: *They complained that he had gone to be a guest with a sinner. They didn't understand that all people are sinners, and that Jesus loves everyone.*

# Theme: A Little Boy's Lunch *(Matthew 14, John 6)*

**1.** Q: Why did the people follow Jesus?

A: *They saw the miracles that he performed.*

**2.** Q: Why was Jesus moved with compassion when he saw the people?

A: *He saw them as sheep having no shepherd.*

**3.** Q: What did Jesus do when the crowd gathered around him?

A: *He taught them and healed the sick people.*

**4.** Q: At evening, what did the disciples ask Jesus to do?

A: *Send the people away so they could buy food.*

**5.** Q: What did Jesus answer?

A: *"They need not depart; give ye them to eat."* (Matthew 14:16)

**6.** Q: Who brought a young lad to Jesus?

A: *Andrew.*

**7.** Q: What was in the boy's lunch?

A: *Five loaves, two fishes.*

**8.** Q: What did Jesus do with the lunch?

A: *He fed the entire crowd of people.*

**9.** Q: How many people shared the boy's lunch?

A: *Five thousand men, plus women and children.*

**10.** Q: Can kids serve God?

A: *Yes! The Bible tells many stories of children who served God.*

**11.** Q: Name some ways that you can serve God.

A: *Pray, love all people, invite friends to church, be a helper, etc.*

**12.** Q: How much food was left after all those thousands of people had eaten?

A: *Twelve baskets full.*

# Theme: Four Men Tear Up a Roof *(Mark 2)*

**1.** Q:  In what town did our story take place?

A:  *Capernaum.*


**2.** Q:  What happened when people heard that Jesus was in town?

A:  *A huge crowd gathered to see and hear him.*


**3.** Q:  What disease did the sick man have?

A:  *Palsy.*


**4.** Q:  What is palsy?

A:  *It is a disease of the nervous system, marked by paralysis, and uncontrolled trembling of the body.*


**5.** Q:  How did the sick man get to Jesus?

A:  *Four friends carried him.*


**6.** Q:  When they got their friend to the house where Jesus was teaching, what problem did they face?

A:  *There were so many people gathered in the house, they could not get in.*


**7.** Q:  What did they do?

A:  *They took the man up on the roof, made a hole through the tiles, and lowered the man to Jesus.*


**8.** Q:  When the man was brought before Jesus, what did Jesus do first?

A:  *He forgave the man's sins.*


**9.** Q:  Why were the scribes upset when Jesus forgave the man's sins?

A: *They knew that only God can forgive sins, and they didn't believe that Jesus was God.*

10. Q: What did Jesus do next for the man?

A: *He healed him.*

11. Q: How do you think the four friends felt when the man was healed?

A: *They were glad that they had cared enough to bring him to Jesus.*

12. Q: Is there ever a problem that is too big for Jesus to handle?

A: *No.*

# Theme: The Good Samaritan *(Luke 10)*

**1.** Q: How did a lawyer try to trick Jesus?

A: *By asking him questions.*

**2.** Q: What question did the lawyer ask to try to justify himself?

A: *"Who is my neighbor?"* (Luke 10:29)

**3.** Q: How did Jesus answer him?

A: *By telling a story.*

**4.** Q: In the story, where was the man going?

A: *To Jericho.*

**5.** Q: What happened as he traveled?

A: *He was jumped by robbers, who hurt him and stripped him.*

**6.** Q: Who came by first and saw what had happened?

A: *A priest.*

**7.** Q: What did he do?

A: *He passed by on the other side.*

**8.** Q: Who came next?

A: *A Levite.*

**9.** Q: What did the Levite do for the wounded man?

A: *Nothing. He also passed by on the other side.*

**10.** Q: Who came next?

A: *A Samaritan.*

**11.** Q: Why could the injured traveler not expect help from the Samaritan?

A: *The Samaritans were not friends with the Jews.*

**12.** Q: What did the Samaritan do?

A: *He had compassion on the man. He gave him first aid, then took him to an inn and paid for his lodging.*

**13.** Q: When he finished the story, what did Jesus say to the lawyer?

A: *"Go, and do thou likewise."* (Luke 10:37)

**14.** Q: What was Jesus teaching us?

A: *We should help anyone, even if they are not our friends.*

# Theme: The Prodigal Son *(Luke 15)*

**1.** Q: Finish Luke 15, verse 11. "A certain man had two_____."

A: *Sons.*

**2.** Q: What did the younger son decide to do?

A: *Leave home and make his own rules.*

**3.** Q: What did he do when he got his inheritance money?

A: *He went to a far country.*

**4.** Q: Why did he go so far from home?

A: *So no one could find him, or so no one could tell him what to do.*

**5.** Q: What kind of life did he live when he got to the far country?

A: *Riotous, or evil.*

**6.** Q: What happened in his new country?

A: *He spent all his money, and a famine came to the land.*

**7.** Q: What was the only job he could find?

A: *Feeding pigs.*

**8.** Q: What did he start thinking about while he was in the pig pen?

A: *Going home to his father.*

**9.** Q: What was his great fear about going home?

A: *He was afraid his father wouldn't want him.*

**10.** Q: What did he decide to do?

A: *He decided to go home and ask his father to hire him as a servant.*

**11.** Q: What did his father say when his son came home?

A: *"You can't be my servant; you are still my son."*

**12.** Q: Who does the father represent, and who does the son represent?

A: *The father is God; the son is us.*

**13.** Q: What did Jesus teach us in this parable?

A: *That God will always love us.*

# Theme: The Resurrection of Jesus
*(Matthew 28, Mark 16, Luke 24, John 20)*

**1.** Q: Name one of the women who went to the tomb.

A: *Mary Magdalene, Mary the mother of James, Salome, Joanna.*

**2.** Q: Why were the women going to the tomb on the morning of the third day?

A: *They were taking spices to anoint Jesus' body.*

**3.** Q: How did the women feel when they saw that the stone had been rolled away from the tomb?

A: *They were perplexed.*

**4.** Q: Why was Mary weeping outside the tomb?

A: *Because they took the Lord away, and she didn't know where he was.*

**5.** Q: What was in the tomb when Peter looked in?

A: *The linen cloths that Jesus had been wearing.*

**6.** Q: Who asked the women why they sought the living among the dead?

A: *An angel.*

**7.** Q: How did the women feel when they saw the angel?

A: *They were frightened.*

**8.** Q: How many days after Jesus was crucified did he rise from the dead?

A: *Three days.*

**9.** Q: What did Jesus tell the women to do after they saw him?

A: *Go tell Peter and the other disciples that he is going to Galilee.*

**10.** Q: What disciple did not believe that Jesus had risen from the dead?

A: *Thomas.*

**11.** Q: What did Thomas say when Jesus showed him his wounds?

A: *"My Lord and my God!"* (John 20:28)

**12.** Q: Who appeared to the men on the road to Emmaus?

A: *Jesus.*

# Theme: The Man on the Steps *(Acts 3)*

**1.** Q: Name the two apostles mentioned in Acts 3.

   A: *Peter and John.*

**2.** Q: Where did they go in today's Bible story?

   A: *To the temple.*

**3.** Q: Why did they go to the temple?

   A: *To pray.*

**4.** Q: What time of day was it?

   A: *The ninth hour, or three o'clock in the afternoon.*

**5.** Q: Whom did Peter and John meet at the gate to the temple?

   A: *A lame man who could not walk.*

**6.** Q: For how long had the man been lame?

   A: *He was lame from birth, and he was over forty years old.*

**7.** Q: What did the man ask Peter and John for?

   A: *He asked for alms, or money.*

**8.** Q: What did Peter say?

   A: *"Silver and gold have I none; but such as I have give I to thee: In the name of Jesus Christ of Nazareth rise up and walk." (Acts 3:6)*

**9.** Q: What happened next?

   A: *Peter took the man by the hand and raised him up. The man was healed immediately and could walk.*

**10.** Q: Who healed the lame man?

A: *Jesus.*

**11.** Q: What did Peter do when a huge crowd gathered around the man that was healed?

A: *He preached to the people about Jesus.*

**12.** Q: What happened when Peter preached?

A: *Many people who heard Peter's message believed. The religious leaders became angry with Peter for preaching in the name of Jesus.*

# Theme: Peter's Jailbreak *(Acts 12)*

**1.** Q: Who was the apostle killed by King Herod?

A: *James, the brother of John.*

**2.** Q: Why did Herod arrest Peter?

A: *He saw that the killing of James pleased the Jews.*

**3.** Q: What did Herod intend to do with Peter?

A: *Kill him after Easter.*

**4.** Q: What did the other disciples do when they learned that Peter was in prison?

A: *They prayed continually.*

**5.** Q: Who released Peter from prison?

A: *An angel.*

**6.** Q: What did Peter think as he followed the angel out of prison?

A: *He thought he was seeing a vision.*

**7.** Q: Where did Peter go when he was released?

A: *To the home of Mary, mother of John Mark.*

**8.** Q: What was happening inside the house when Peter arrived?

A: *Many disciples were gathered, praying for Peter.*

**9.** Q: Who came to the door when Peter knocked?

A: *Rhoda.*

**10.** Q: How did the disciples respond when Rhoda told them that Peter was at the door?

    A: *They didn't believe her.*

**11.** Q: Should they have believed her?

    A: *Yes. God had promised to answer their prayers.*

**12.** Q: Does God answer prayer today?

    A: *Yes.*

**13.** Q: What did Herod do when he learned of Peter's escape?

    A: *He had the keepers of the prison put to death.*

**14.** Q: What do you think the disciples learned from Peter's experience?

    A: *That God answers prayer, even when it seems impossible.*

# Theme: Midnight Jailbreak *(Acts 16)*

**1.** Q: Name the city in which our Bible story took place.

A: *Philippi.*

**2.** Q: Name the principal characters in our Bible story.

A: *Paul and Silas.*

**3.** Q: Why did Paul and Silas travel to so many different cities?

A: *They were preaching the Gospel of Jesus Christ.*

**4.** Q: What did Lydia do after she heard the Gospel and was saved?

A: *She was baptized.*

**5.** Q: Who was the young woman who followed Paul and Silas?

A: *She was a woman who was possessed with evil spirits and told fortunes.*

**6.** Q: What did Paul do when the woman had followed them for several days?

A: *He commanded the evil spirits to come out of the woman in the name of Jesus Christ.*

**7.** Q: What did the woman's slave owners do to Paul and Silas?

A: *They beat them severely, then threw them into prison.*

**8.** Q: What did Paul and Silas do in prison?

A: *They sang praises to God.*

**9.** Q: Why do *you* think they didn't complain about being thrown into prison?

A: *Accept any valid answer to this thought question.*

**10.** Q: What happened at midnight?

A: *A tremendous earthquake struck; the prison doors were opened; the shackles fell off the prisoners.*

**11.** Q: When the jailer came into the prison, what important question did he ask Paul and Silas?

A: *"What must I do to be saved?"*

**12.** Q: What answer did Paul and Silas give?

A: *"Believe on the Lord Jesus Christ, and thou shalt be saved."* (Acts 16:31)

**13.** Q: What did the jailer and his family do after they were saved?

A: *They were baptized.*

# PART FOUR
## *Patterns*

The following patterns may be enlarged and copied in several ways. The easiest option is to take the book to a copy shop to have it done, based on the charts that follow. If you prefer enlarging the patterns yourself, you may either use an overhead projector and "guesstimate" the size, or you may use a copy machine capable of enlarging to at least 155%. For patterns larger than 155%, enlarge to the 155% limit and recopy the copied pattern again until the correct percentage is reached.

| Figure(s) | Game Titles | Small Board | Large Board |
|---|---|---|---|
| 1 | Zonk! | 100% | 230% |
| (Use bear from fig.78) | Rabbit Hunt | 70% | 205% |
| 2 | Rabbit Hunt | 100% | 265% |
| 3 | Rabbit Hunt | 100% | 225% |
| 4, 5, 6 | Survival | 85% | 200% |
| 7 | Survival | 140% | 350% |
| 8 | Survival | 100% | 200% |
| (Use circle from fig.1) | Survival | 100% | 250% |
| 9 | Matchmaker | 135% | 220% |
| 10, 11, 12, 13, 14 | Matchmaker | 100% | 200% |
| (Use circle from fig.1) | Matchmaker | 100% | 230% |
| 15 | Dinosaur Daze | 170% | |
| 16 | Dinosaur Daze | 200% | |
| 17, 18, 19, 20 | Dinosaur Daze | 140% | |
| 21 | Dinosaur Daze | 150% | |
| 22 | Dinosaur Daze | 140% | |
| 23 | Dinosaur Daze | 250% | |
| 24 | Dinosaur Daze | 140% | |
| 25, 26 | Leap Frog | 100% | 220% |
| 27, 28 | Leap Frog | 90% | 225% |
| 29 | Double Dip | 100% | 225% |
| 30 (all scoops) | Double Dip | 100% | 225% |
| 31, 32, 33, 34, 35, 36 | Sea Monster | 125% | |
| 37 | Sky War | 140% | |
| 38, 39 | Sky War | 95% | |

| Figure(s) | Game Titles | Small Board | Large Board |
|---|---|---|---|
| 40 | Sky War | 110% | 260% |
| 41, 42, 43 | The Lost Dutchman | 110% | 230% |
| 44 | The Lost Dutchman | 100% | 250% |
| 45 | The Lost Dutchman | 100% | 200% |
| 46 | The Lost Dutchman | 100% | 200% |
| 47, 48 | The Lost Dutchman | 100% | 260% |
| 49, 50, 51, 52 | The Lost Dutchman | 110% | 230% |
| 53 | Magic Squares | 170% | 325% |
| (Use circle from fig.1) | Magic Squares | 115% | 250% |
| (Use bonus from fig.11) | Magic Squares | 115% | 250% |
| 54 (all wanted posters) | Good Guys, Bad Guys | 125% | 300% |
| 55, 56, 57 | Good Guys, Bad Guys | 100% | 270% |
| 58, 59, 60, 61 | Good Guys, Bad Guys | 110% | |
| 62 | The Green Machine | 580% | |
| 63 | Bible Treasure | 85% | 225% |
| 64 | Bible Treasure | 100% | 255% |
| 65, 66, 67 | Bible Treasure | 110% | 250% |
| 68 | Busy Bees | 140% | 400% |
| 69, 70 | Busy Bees | 115% | 300% |
| 71 | Busy Bees | 180% | 450% |
| 72, 73, 74, 75 | Build-A-Bug | 170% | 420% |
| 76 | Build-A-Bug | 240% | 600% |
| 77 | Chasing Butterflies | 100% | 210% |
| 78 | Hungry Bears | 120% | 290% |
| 79 | Hungry Bears | 90% | 215% |
| 80 | Chasing Butterflies | 100% | 235% |
| 81 | Chasing Butterflies | 100% | 210% |
| 82 | All Games Award | 100% | 200% |

figure 2

figure 1

figure 3

figure 4

figure 5

figure 6

figure 7

172

*figure 8*

*figure 9*

*figure 10*

*figure 11*

figure 12

figure 13

figure 14

175

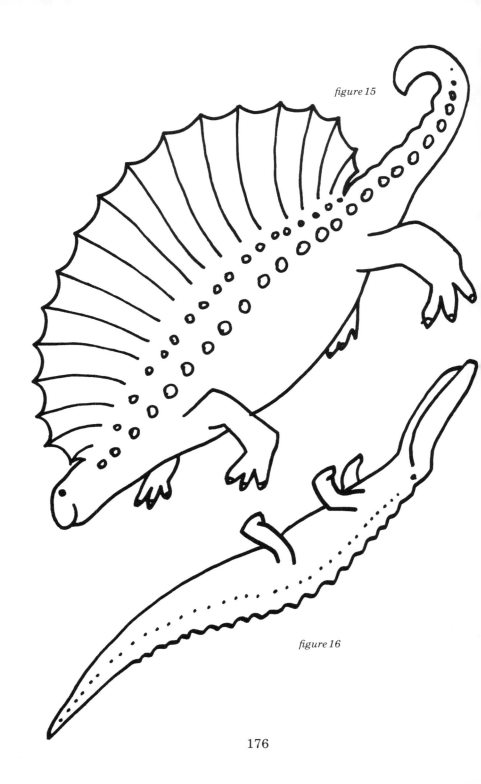

figure 15

figure 16

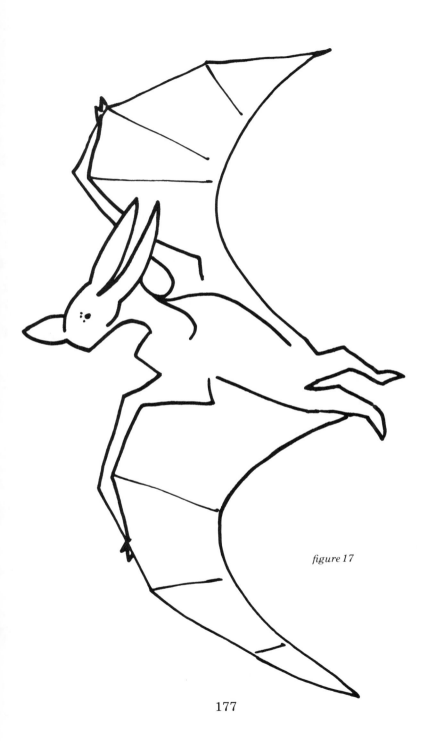

*figure 17*

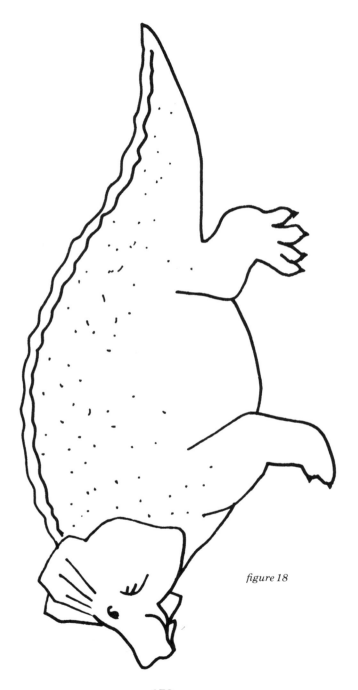

*figure 18*

figure 19

179

*figure 20*

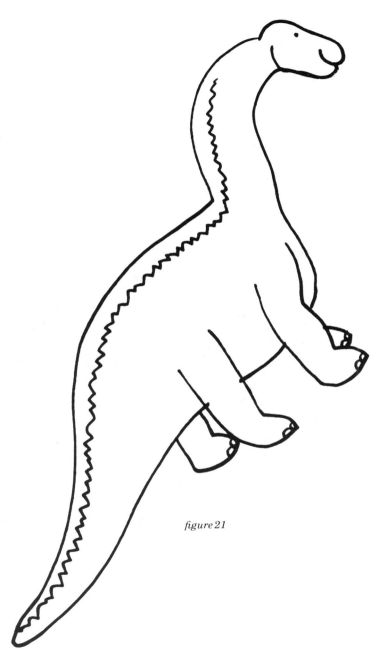

*figure 21*

*figure 22*

figure 23

figure 24

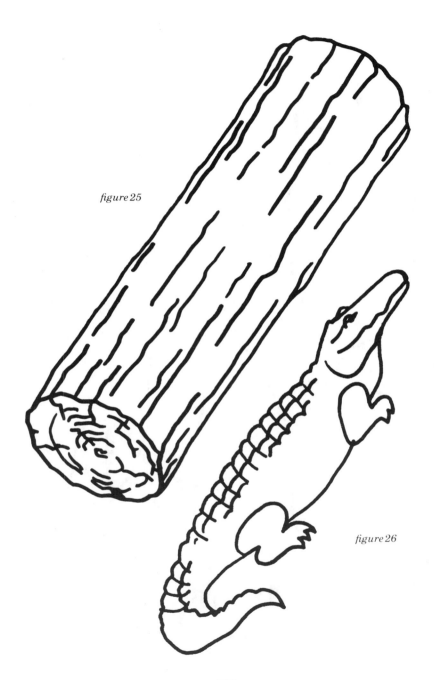

*figure 25*

*figure 26*

*figure 27*

*figure 28*

*figure 29*

185

*figure* 30

figure 31

figure 32

figure 33

*figure 34*

*figure 35*

*figure 36*

*figure 37*

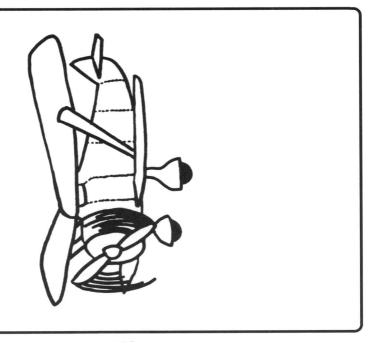

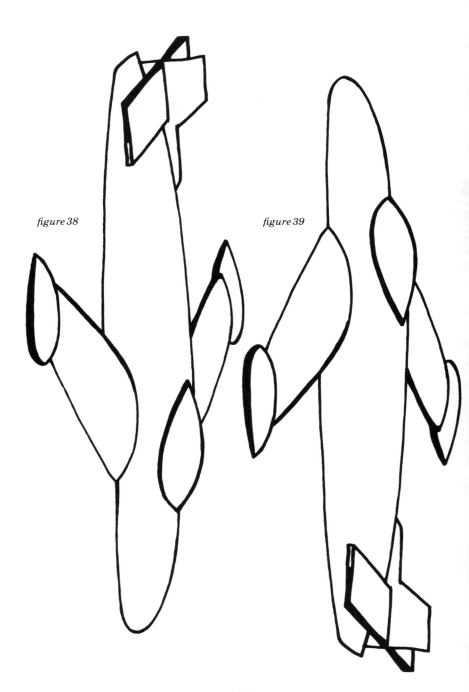

figure 38

figure 39

figure 40

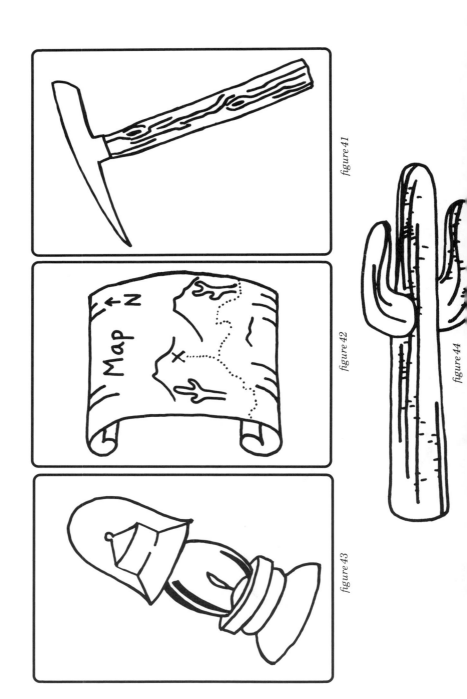

figure 41

figure 42

figure 43

figure 44

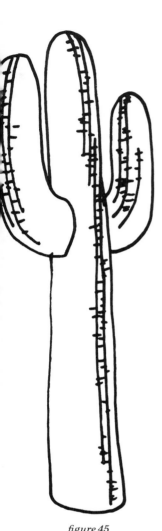

figure 45

figure 46

figure 47

194

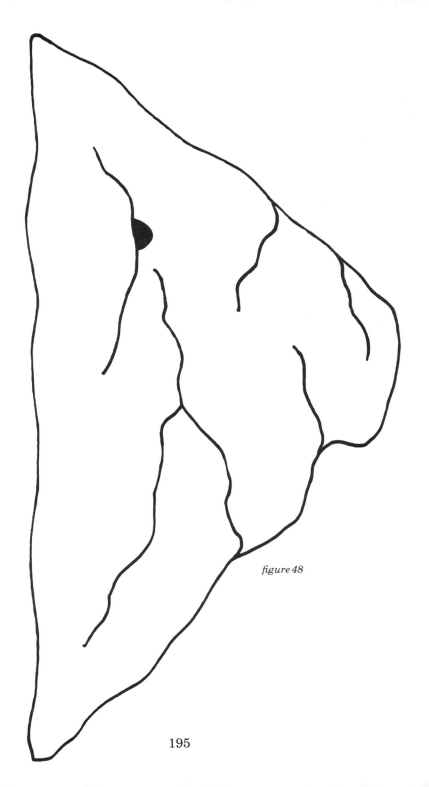

*figure 48*

*figure 49*

# STEPPED ON RATTLESNAKE!

# LOSE A TURN.

*figure 50*

# CHOOSE ONE!

*figure 51*

# LOST IN DESERT!

# LOSE YOUR

*figure 52*

*figure 53*

**WANTED**

**$400**
**REWARD**

MAKE 3

**WANTED**

**$500**
**REWARD**

MAKE 5

**WANTED**

**$100**
**REWARD**

MAKE 5

**WANTED**

**$300**
**REWARD**

MAKE 5

**WANTED**

**$750**
**REWARD**

MAKE 2

*figure 54*

**WANTED**

**$200**
**REWARD**

MAKE 5

**WANTED**

**$50**
**REWARD**

MAKE 5

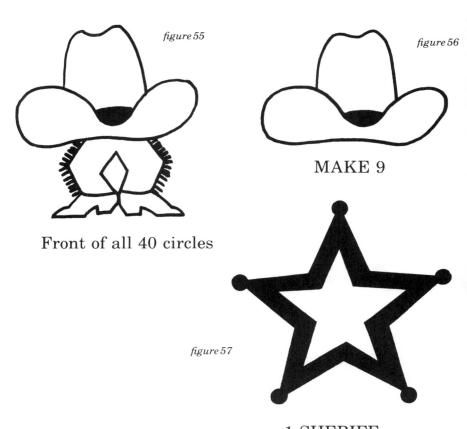

figure 55

figure 56

MAKE 9

Front of all 40 circles

figure 57

1 SHERIFF

figure 58

*figure 59*

*figure 60*

*figure 61*

199

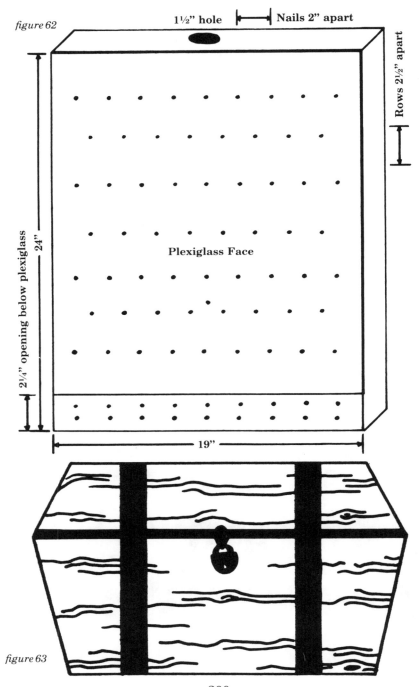

*figure 62*

1½" hole

Nails 2" apart

Rows 2½" apart

24"

2¼" opening below plexiglass

**Plexiglass Face**

19"

*figure 63*

200

Sorry!

figure 64

figure 65

figure 66

figure 67

*figure 68*

*figure 69*

*figure 70*

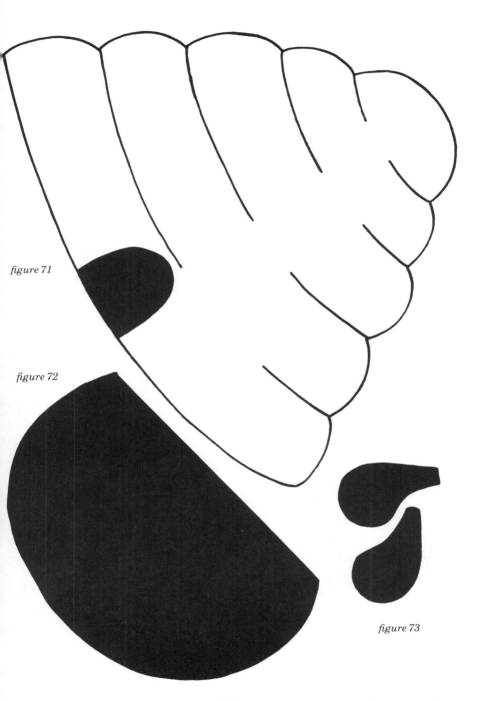

*figure 71*

*figure 72*

*figure 73*

203

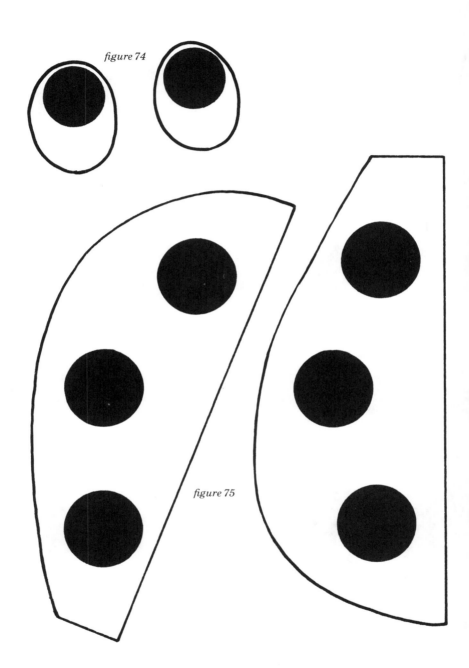

figure 74

figure 75

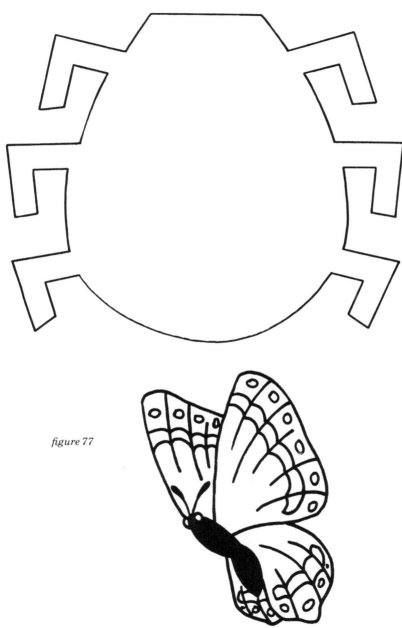

*figure 76*

*figure 77*

*figure 78*

*figure 79*

*figure 80*

*figure 81*

figure 82

**BOYS    GIRLS**

# A Final Word

I trust that you have enjoyed reading the game ideas in this book, and that many of the ideas will be useful to you in your own children's ministry. The Bible games presented in this book have been loved by young people everywhere we go, and I think that your students will enjoy them also.

Please let me say this — if you intend to use some of the Bible games in this book, begin making them now. Start making your very first Bible game now, and plan to use it in class this week. Set a goal to have a second game finished in two weeks, and use it the third week. Don't wait; begin making and using the games right away!

Many times we go into churches and conduct teacher-training seminars. One of the sessions deals with making and using Bible games similar to those presented in this book. I watch the teachers as they take notes, writing down the game ideas as they are presented.

Often we go back to a church the next year, and we see the teachers using the Bible games that they have made. It's good to see the ideas being used. But, many times, we go back the second year, and some of the teachers have not made any of the games at all! They were all excited, and had every intention of making and using the Bible games, but somehow, they just never got around to actually doing it!

Set some goals right now. Determine today which Bible game you will make first, and when you will have it finished. Begin working on it right away. As you start using that first game in class, start working on your second. Make plans for a third. In just a few weeks, you'll have a whole library of exciting Bible games for your students to enjoy. Your Sunday School class or Junior Church will never be the same.

One more thing: when you make your games, make them look as good as they possibly can. Almost every game in this book is completely homemade, yet none of them look shoddy or second-rate! The children you minister to deserve your very best! And so does your Lord! Once you make the games, be sure to make the storage envelopes and store them properly. They'll last for years!

God bless you in your ministry to children!

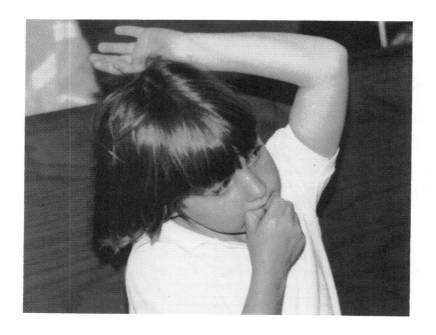

# ABOUT THE AUTHOR

Ed Dunlop has worked in children's ministries full-time for over 16 years. Known to thousands of children across America simply as "Mr. Ed," he is a children's evangelist, conducting Kids' Crusades in local churches. Ed also conducts teacher-training seminars, speaks at junior camps, and presents visualized drug and alcohol programs in public elementary and junior high schools. His ministry involves ventriloquism, Gospel magic, blacklight effects, and a variety of other visual media.

Ed graduated from Pacific Coast Baptist Bible College in 1975, at the age of 19. He has served as Christian Education Director in churches in California, Arizona, and Tennessee.

Ed and his wife Janice make their home in Ringgold, Georgia. They have three children, Rebecca, Steven, and Phillip.

If the "active learning" approach of TEACHING WITH BIBLE GAMES was popular with your church children, then they'll be equally enthused about this collection of 52 "hands on" activity lessons:

# NO EXPERIENCE NECESSARY!
## by
## Elaine Clanton Harpine

This year-long program teaches children about church worship through activity workstations relevant to each part of a service: the Call to Worship, Affirmation of Faith, Offering, Sermon, Witness to the World, Prayer, and the Benediction. Each workstation is set up with supplies and instructions, allowing the children to work at their own pace. All activities are easy to understand and do. The book includes reproducible instructions and sign-up sheets, patterns, illustrations and photos. This program may be used for children's church or Sunday school— or even as an idea book to supplement an existing children's program.

### Sample activities include:

- Building a children's church
- Making "stained glass" windows from tissue paper
- Writing and presenting a worship service
- Street mime and clown ministry

*Full of tested and proven activities for groups of 4- to 12-year-olds. Lessons are adaptable for all Protestant denominations. A plus for Christian education workers!*

# ORDER FORM

**MERIWETHER PUBLISHING LTD.**
**P.O. BOX 7710**
**COLORADO SPRINGS, CO 80933**
**TELEPHONE: (719) 594-4422**

*Please send me the following books:*

_____**Teaching With Bible Games #CC-B108**  **$10.95**
by Ed Dunlop
*20 "kid-tested" contests for Christian education*

_____**No Experience Necessary! #CC-B107**  **$12.95**
by Elaine Clanton Harpine
*A "learn by doing" guide for creating children's worship*

_____**Where Does God Live? #CC-B189**  **$8.95**
by Ted Lazicki
*Fifty-eight children's sermons for worship*

_____**The Official Sunday School Teachers**
**Handbook #CC-B152**  **$9.95**
by Joanne Owens
*An indispensable aid for anyone involved in Sunday school activities*

_____**You Can Do Christian Puppets #CC-B196**  **$9.95**
by Bea Carlton
*A basic guide to Christian puppetry*

_____**Celebrating Special Days in the Church**
**School Year #CC-B146**  **$9.95**
by Judy Gattis Smith
*Liturgies and participation activities for children*

**These and other fine Meriwether Publishing books are available at
your local Christian bookstore or direct from the publisher. Use the
handy order form on this page.**

*I understand that I may return any book
for a full refund if not satisfied.*

NAME: _____

ORGANIZATION NAME: _____

ADDRESS: _____

CITY: _____ STATE: _____ ZIP: _____

PHONE: _____

☐ **Check Enclosed**
☐ **Visa or Mastercard #** _____

             *Expiration*
*Signature:* _____ *Date:* _____

*(required for Visa/Mastercard orders)*

**COLORADO RESIDENTS:** Please add 3% sales tax.
**SHIPPING:** Include $1.95 for the first book and 50¢ for each additional book ordered.

☐ *Please send me a copy of your complete catalog of books and plays.*

# ORDER FORM

**MERIWETHER PUBLISHING LTD.**
**P.O. BOX 7710**
**COLORADO SPRINGS, CO 80933**
**TELEPHONE: (719) 594-4422**

*Please send me the following books:*

_____**Teaching With Bible Games #CC-B108**          **$10.95**
by **Ed Dunlop**
*20 "kid-tested" contests for Christian education*

_____**No Experience Necessary! #CC-B107**          **$12.95**
by **Elaine Clanton Harpine**
*A "learn by doing" guide for creating children's worship*

_____**Where Does God Live? #CC-B189**          **$8.95**
by **Ted Lazicki**
*Fifty-eight children's sermons for worship*

_____**The Official Sunday School Teachers**
**Handbook #CC-B152**          **$9.95**
by **Joanne Owens**
*An indispensable aid for anyone involved in Sunday school activities*

_____**You Can Do Christian Puppets #CC-B196**          **$9.95**
by **Bea Carlton**
*A basic guide to Christian puppetry*

_____**Celebrating Special Days in the Church**
**School Year #CC-B146**          **$9.95**
by **Judy Gattis Smith**
*Liturgies and participation activities for children*

**These and other fine Meriwether Publishing books are available at your local Christian bookstore or direct from the publisher. Use the handy order form on this page.**

*I understand that I may return any book*
*for a full refund if not satisfied.*

NAME: _____

ORGANIZATION NAME: _____

ADDRESS: _____

CITY: _____ STATE: _____ ZIP: _____

PHONE: _____

☐ **Check Enclosed**
☐ **Visa or Mastercard #** _____
                                                    *Expiration*
*Signature:* _____  *Date:* _____
          *(required for Visa/Mastercard orders)*

**COLORADO RESIDENTS:** Please add 3% sales tax.
**SHIPPING:** Include $1.95 for the first book and 50¢ for each additional book ordered.

☐ *Please send me a copy of your complete catalog of books and plays.*